You Are
the One

To , Cengal B.
May this help us
thru difficult times, as
we spend exciting years
together, with children,
and growth in all
aspects of our
lives---
Love, Ron

You Are the One

Living Fully, Living Free
through Affirmative Prayer

Mary M. Jaeger
Kathleen Juline

with selections from the writings of
ERNEST HOLMES

SCIENCE OF MIND PUBLICATIONS
Los Angeles, California

Acknowledgements

The authors wish to acknowledge the founder of the Science of Mind philosophy, Ernest Holmes (1887-1960), whose teachings provide the basis for this workbook. His profoundly beneficial influence in the world continues to grow, and we are grateful to him.

Particular recognition is due John S. Niendorff, our editor and project coordinator. His expert help in all aspects of the editing and production of this book was invaluable. As a result of his highly significant contribution, You Are the One was greatly improved in terms of clarity and effectiveness. John gave unstintingly of his time and of his outstanding talent, and we thank him.

We also thank Dr. Kouji Nakata, Dean of Ernest Holmes College, for his enthusiastic involvement in the creation of You Are the One. Kouji brought a sensitivity to the conceptualization of this book that much enhanced its strength and cohesiveness as a teaching tool. Gary Lister made additional creative contributions, and we are grateful to him for his support. Further, we say a special thank-you to the Science of Mind ministers who graciously read the manuscript and made excellent suggestions. Also, many members of the staff of United Church of Religious Science headquarters participated in a variety of ways, and we thank them.

We appreciate everyone's valuable help. Working together as a team has been fun and fulfilling.

First Edition — November 1988
Copyright © 1988 by Science of Mind Publications

Printed in the United States of America

Published by
SCIENCE OF MIND PUBLICATIONS
3251 West Sixth Street
P.O. Box 75127
Los Angeles, California 90075

Photographs by Johnny De Jesus

Book design by Deborah Daly

CONTENTS

WELCOME TO A NEW LIFE

In using *You Are the One,* you are beginning the journey toward a new way of living. What awaits you? The extraordinary discovery that through the use of affirmative prayer you have the ability to change your life for the better, to bring about any good you desire.

As you progress in this journey, you will find your life being gradually and positively transformed. Wonderful events you never before thought possible will come to pass, as you enter into a greater awareness of your spiritual nature and apply that awareness to your daily experience.

If using affirmative prayer is a new concept for you, be open to it. We believe you will find it amazingly effective. If it is not new to you, you will nevertheless benefit tremendously by using this workbook, for it encourages the thoughtful and focused application of a simple but profound spiritual practice which leads to untold reward.

Remember, *you are the one!* You can change your life — through becoming aware of your unity with an infinite Source and consciously directing the creative Power within you. Begin your journey to a new you — *now!*

INTRODUCTION

"If you will take time daily to sense the presence of Life within you, to believe in it, to accept it, . . . undesirable experiences which you have known will gradually disappear and something new will be born — a bigger, better, and more perfect you. You will pass from lack and want into greater freedom, from fear into faith. From a sense of being alone, you will pass into the realization of oneness with everything, and you will rejoice."

These words, written by Dr. Ernest Holmes, founder of the Science of Mind philosophy, convey the essence of what this workbook is designed to help you do.

You Are the One is based on the Science of Mind philosophy, which teaches that when you establish a deep awareness of your unity with the Presence and Power of God, and apply that awareness to your specific needs, a change in the circumstances of your life occurs. You begin to experience a greater good than you have ever known before.

This workbook focuses particularly on the Science of Mind viewpoint that all problems are the result of limiting or negative beliefs and that problems will disappear when these beliefs are eliminated and new, life-affirming beliefs are accepted.

What Is Affirmative Prayer?

The Science of Mind — which is based on ideas that are thousands of years old and is also illumined by modern understanding — includes a powerful method for resolving specific problems and bringing forth greater good. Dr. Holmes called this method *spiritual mind treatment* or — the term we have chosen to use in this workbook — *affirmative prayer*. Affirmative prayer involves a deep understanding that the good of God is everywhere present and is the truth right now about a specific situation. This understanding, which affirms that a desired good already *is*, replaces any prior belief in lack or limitation and establishes a new, more positive belief in the mind of the person praying. This new belief then takes outer form through the activity of the Universal Law of Mind.

Experience has shown that one of the most effective ways to understand and use affirmative prayer is to separate it into five stages: recognition, unification, realization, thanksgiving, and release. The purpose of doing so is not to set up a rigid formula but rather to provide a framework for the clear, constructive acceptance of a desired good. That five-stage framework forms the basis for this workbook.

How to Use This Workbook

The key to deriving the most benefit from *You Are the One* is to commit yourself wholeheartedly to being open-minded, patient, receptive, and persistent. Above all, be convinced that the good you are seeking will emerge.

Be willing to expand your thinking. Take an honest look at yourself, acknowledge limiting beliefs when you discover them, and then release them. Have the courage to move forward into the new and the unknown. Let yourself begin to live the way you really want to — free from unhappiness, pain, lack, fear, conflict, worry. Resolve to take charge of your life and open yourself to the infinite possibilities that await you.

Let this workbook serve as a tool for making powerful, inner changes in yourself. Write in it; read it; carry it around with you; work with it; use it. The more you do so, the more you will benefit.

Into Action

Begin by turning to the self-assessment section, "Where Am I Now?" (page 14) The exercises in this section will help you determine your starting point among the twelve major areas of life-experience covered in *You Are the One* — money, health, employment, marriage, childraising, parents, friendship, growing older, addiction, death and dying, emotional well-being, and life direction.

After selecting the area you want to start with, go to the workbook section which deals with that area, where you will identify the specific problem you wish to resolve. In this section you will learn about the power of your thoughts, feelings, and attitudes — your beliefs. You will also explore your current beliefs and work on eliminating negative ones. Your goal in doing these exercises is to expand your thinking and to build a foundation that will enable you to accept a greater good.

The next section, "Creating My New Life," is the heart of *You Are the One*. Here you develop your own personal affirmative prayer to resolve the particular problem you have chosen to deal with. Using this affirmative prayer, you will begin to make profound changes in your beliefs, focusing no longer on limitation but, instead, on your unity with the Presence and Power of God. You will apply spiritual Truth to your personal concern, thus preparing the way for the Universal Law of Mind, acting on these new beliefs, to create the good you desire.

Other parts of each workbook section include valuable suggestions and guidance that will help you continue to benefit from affirmative prayer. They also offer you an opportunity to record the positive changes that take place in your life as you apply affirmative prayer to your specific problems.

You may wish to deal with one problem at a time or with several simultaneously. Either approach is fine. Use the workbook in any way that best suits your needs and personality, keeping in mind that no problem is too great or too small to be resolved through affirmative prayer. Whatever your specific concern may be, even if it seems ordinary, it is an appropriate one to work with.

A Comment on Workbook Terminology

"When we use the word God we are saluting the Divine Presence in each other and in everything — the beauty that sees and imagines and paints the glory of a sunset or the softness of an early dawn, the aroma of the rose, the enthusiasm of the child at play, the intelligence of the philosopher, the worshipful attitude of the devotee. This is all God."

These words of Dr. Holmes beautifully describe that inexpressible Something which people worldwide have believed in and sought after and which mystics, poets, philosophers, and sages throughout the centuries have experienced directly through intuition. Many other descriptions have been written in an attempt to capture all that God is, and a variety of different names for deity have been used — Spirit, Father, Divine Mother, First Cause, Ultimate Reality, Infinite Intelligence, or Absolute Truth. In *You Are the One,* we have chosen to use the words Presence and Power to refer to God, since these are terms favored by Dr. Holmes and also since they provide a good way to distinguish the two complementary aspects of God, the personal and the impersonal.

Spiritual philosophies throughout the ages, including the Science of Mind, have recognized both a personal and an impersonal aspect to Divinity: a Presence to believe in and a Power to use. The Presence of God — the personal aspect — is the guiding Spirit behind all that is. It is the "knowing" side of life. The Power of God — the impersonal aspect — is the automatic, responsive activity of Spirit. It is the "doing" side of life. This doing side of life — the Power of God — operates in accordance with an exact and unfailing Universal Law of Cause and Effect, which we refer to in this workbook as the Universal Law of Mind. This Universal Law of Mind, which draws upon an infinite Intelligence, creates in accordance with the mold or pattern presented to it. The Law of Cause and Effect works in this way: a person's thoughts, feelings, and attitudes provide the *cause,* while the *effect* is that person's experience in the outer world.

The greater your recognition of the Divine Presence in and through everything, especially within yourself, and the more you let this recognition replace prior beliefs in limitation or disharmony, the more you will discover that good flows in increasing measure into your life, as the Universal Law of Mind acts on the new beliefs you are forming.

One way to build such a recognition is to focus on the qualities of God, becoming aware of them in the world around you and also within your own nature. A number of these Divine qualities are highlighted in the workbook — such as Abundance and Support in relation to money, Freedom and Strength in relation to addiction, and so on. Contemplating these various Divine qualities will help you enlarge your concept of God and build a greater awareness of God's Presence within you.

As a result of using affirmative prayer, you will discover that a radiant and perfect Life is living through you, and you will automatically express more of the Love, Peace, Joy, Wisdom, and Harmony that flow unceasingly from God.

Sample Affirmative Prayers

The following affirmative prayers will not only provide you with guidance in creating your own as you work with *You Are the One* but will also offer inspiration as you begin your new adventure of living fully and living free through affirmative prayer.

I Have Great Expectations

I recognize the existence of an infinite Presence and Power everywhere in the universe, ever available and constantly active.

I know that there is nothing opposed to or separate from this one perfect Life and that I am an essential part of it. I know it lives and expresses through me, now and always.

In this deep conviction, I declare that happiness, success, harmony, and fulfillment are mine, in every area of my experience. Letting go of any belief in limitation, lack, or discord, I am filled with complete assurance that an abundance of all good is mine, now. I know there is no end to the outpouring of God's Love into my life, and I am richly blessed in every way.

Opening myself now to an ever expanding good, I joyfully receive this great outpouring and give thanks for it.

I now release this affirmative prayer, confident of obtaining the results I desire. I allow the Universal Law of Mind to bring forth for me a new experience of joyous living.

I Enter into a Larger Life

I recognize the limitless resources of the Divine Presence and the perfect activity of Divine Power.

Knowing that as a spiritual being I am unified with this Presence and Power, I now affirm that today I look out upon a broader horizon.

Across all the experiences I may have had which were limited or unpleasant I now see the rosy hue of a new dawn. Letting go of that which is little, I enter into a larger concept of life. Dropping all fear, I entertain faith. Realizing that every form of uncertainty is the result of my seeing only in part, I open myself to that which is Wholeness. which is ever greater and greater. Today I am open to the breadth and the height and the depth of a loving Presence and immutable Power, which creates in my life right now a wonderful new good.

I gratefully accept this expanding good, in every form it takes.

Releasing this prayer to the Universal Law of Mind, I allow all concern to fade away. I let go and let God.

In reading these affirmative prayers, you may have felt a shift in your attitude toward some current situation in your life — a feeling of greater freedom, lightness, or unburdening. You may also have been filled with peace and a joyful sense of expansion. These are the kinds of feelings that will arise within you as you create and work with your own affirmative prayers. You will feel lifted out of your problem and you will be completely convinced that all is well.

And remarkable results will follow.

WHERE AM I NOW?

This section consists of twelve self-assessment exercises to help you identify specific problems in the areas listed below. Use these exercises, on the pages indicated, to begin creating positive changes in your life.

MONEY

Use the following list to identify your problem areas in regard to money. After you select statements that fit your circumstances, rate the intensity of each problem by circling a number on the scale from 1 to 5, letting "1" equal a minor problem and "5" equal a major problem.

My salary isn't enough to live on.	1	2	3	4	5
I spend too much money.	1	2	3	4	5
I have problems borrowing money.	1	2	3	4	5
I can't support my family.	1	2	3	4	5
I never have enough money.	1	2	3	4	5
My credit rating is poor.	1	2	3	4	5
I have a problem getting raises.	1	2	3	4	5
I can't afford the things my children need.	1	2	3	4	5
I can't save money.	1	2	3	4	5
I'm behind in child support payments.	1	2	3	4	5
I'm facing bankruptcy.	1	2	3	4	5
I gamble too much.	1	2	3	4	5
I can't pay my bills.	1	2	3	4	5
I've made bad investments.	1	2	3	4	5
I'm worried about providing for retirement.	1	2	3	4	5
I'm afraid of poverty.	1	2	3	4	5
I have too many debts.	1	2	3	4	5
I can't pay for my schooling.	1	2	3	4	5
Other_____ (list other problem areas)	1	2	3	4	5
_____	1	2	3	4	5

If you circled 3, 4, or 5 for any problem, turn to the workbook section on money (page 29), where you will find exercises to help you change what you are experiencing.

HEALTH

Use the following list to identify your problem areas in regard to health. After you select statements that fit your circumstances, rate the intensity of each problem by circling a number on the scale from 1 to 5, letting "1" equal a minor problem and "5" equal a major problem.

I'm always catching a cold or the flu.	1	2	3	4	5
I have problems with my weight.	1	2	3	4	5
My energy level is low.	1	2	3	4	5
I have difficulty sleeping.	1	2	3	4	5
I'm afraid to have the surgery I need.	1	2	3	4	5
I have many allergies.	1	2	3	4	5
My sexual functioning is poor.	1	2	3	4	5
I suffer with excessive pain.	1	2	3	4	5
I have a life-threatening illness.	1	2	3	4	5
I am under treatment for cancer.	1	2	3	4	5
I have trouble breathing.	1	2	3	4	5
I'm afraid I'll inherit family illnesses.	1	2	3	4	5
I have severe headaches.	1	2	3	4	5
Arthritis is crippling me.	1	2	3	4	5
I have serious digestive problems.	1	2	3	4	5
I only have a short time to live.	1	2	3	4	5
I'm not in good health.	1	2	3	4	5
I have problems with my nerves.	1	2	3	4	5
Other_____	1	2	3	4	5
(list other problem areas)					
_____	1	2	3	4	5

If you circled 3, 4, or 5 for any problem, turn to the workbook section on health (page 43), where you will find exercises to help you change what you are experiencing.

EMPLOYMENT

Use the following list to identify your problem areas in regard to employment or business. After you select statements that fit your circumstances, rate the intensity of each problem by circling a number on the scale from 1 to 5, letting "1" equal a minor problem and "5" equal a major problem.

My job conflicts with family life.	1	2	3	4	5
I experience discrimination at work.	1	2	3	4	5
My job is too stressful.	1	2	3	4	5
I don't like the competition at work.	1	2	3	4	5
I'm overlooked for promotions.	1	2	3	4	5
I lack career direction.	1	2	3	4	5
I have poor job benefits.	1	2	3	4	5
My salary is not adequate or equitable.	1	2	3	4	5
I don't like my job.	1	2	3	4	5
I'm not able to be creative in my job.	1	2	3	4	5
I can't find good employees.	1	2	3	4	5
I'm afraid of job interviews.	1	2	3	4	5
I have conflicts with my coworkers/boss.	1	2	3	4	5
I am sexually harassed at work.	1	2	3	4	5
My job is hazardous.	1	2	3	4	5
I'm out of work.	1	2	3	4	5
My business is failing.	1	2	3	4	5
I have problems with child care.	1	2	3	4	5
Other_____	1	2	3	4	5
(list other problem areas)					
_____	1	2	3	4	5

If you circled 3, 4, or 5 for any problem, turn to the workbook section on employment (page 57), where you will find exercises to help you change what you are experiencing.

SELF-ASSESSMENT

MARRIAGE

Use the following list to identify your problem areas in regard to marriage or a primary relationship. After you select statements that fit your circumstances, rate the intensity of each problem by circling a number on the scale from 1 to 5, letting "1" equal a minor problem and "5" equal a major problem.

We have communication problems.	1	2	3	4	5
We don't agree on how to spend money.	1	2	3	4	5
My partner dominates me.	1	2	3	4	5
I have trouble with my in-laws.	1	2	3	4	5
I don't feel loved anymore.	1	2	3	4	5
My partner abuses me.	1	2	3	4	5
We fight a great deal of the time.	1	2	3	4	5
We disagree on childraising.	1	2	3	4	5
I think my partner is having an affair.	1	2	3	4	5
We're growing apart.	1	2	3	4	5
I can't find the right mate.	1	2	3	4	5
We don't like the same kinds of people.	1	2	3	4	5
Our sex life is dull.	1	2	3	4	5
We spend very little time together.	1	2	3	4	5
My partner's job always comes first.	1	2	3	4	5
I don't feel appreciated.	1	2	3	4	5
Our relationship is boring.	1	2	3	4	5
We have serious religious differences.	1	2	3	4	5
Other_____	1	2	3	4	5
(list other problem areas)					
_____	1	2	3	4	5

If you circled 3, 4, or 5 for any problem, turn to the workbook section on marriage (page 71), where you will find exercises to help you change what you are experiencing.

CHILDRAISING

Use the following list to identify your problem areas in regard to childraising. After you select statements that fit your circumstances, rate the intensity of each problem by circling a number on the scale from 1 to 5, letting "1" equal a minor problem and "5" equal a major problem.

I'm afraid my child is using drugs.	1	2	3	4	5
I don't have enough time with my children.	1	2	3	4	5
I don't know how to set limits.	1	2	3	4	5
I can't provide for my child's needs.	1	2	3	4	5
Raising children alone is hard for me.	1	2	3	4	5
My child is having problems with school.	1	2	3	4	5
My visitation rights are too limited.	1	2	3	4	5
I don't have any time for myself.	1	2	3	4	5
I can't talk with my child about sex.	1	2	3	4	5
I'm not a good parent.	1	2	3	4	5
I can't handle my child anymore.	1	2	3	4	5
I can't cope with my child's illness.	1	2	3	4	5
Our marriage is stressed by the new baby.	1	2	3	4	5
My spouse and I disagree on childraising.	1	2	3	4	5
I don't want my children to leave me.	1	2	3	4	5
My children and I argue too much.	1	2	3	4	5
I can't get my children to study.	1	2	3	4	5
I'm afraid to discipline my child.	1	2	3	4	5
Other_____	1	2	3	4	5
(list other problem areas)					
_____	1	2	3	4	5

If you circled 3, 4, or 5 for any problem, turn to the workbook section on childraising (page 85), where you will find exercises to help you change what you are experiencing.

PARENTS

Use the following list to identify your problem areas in regard to your relationship with your parents. After you select statements that fit your circumstances, rate the intensity of each problem by circling a number on the scale from 1 to 5, letting "1" equal a minor problem and "5" equal a major problem.

My parents are a financial burden.	1	2	3	4	5
I'm concerned about my parent's illness.	1	2	3	4	5
My parents treat me like a child.	1	2	3	4	5
I don't like my parent's new spouse.	1	2	3	4	5
Nothing I do satisfies my parents.	1	2	3	4	5
I have to deal with an alcoholic parent.	1	2	3	4	5
My parents are meddling in my life.	1	2	3	4	5
I can't forgive my parents for some things.	1	2	3	4	5
My parents are too dependent on me.	1	2	3	4	5
I need to put my parent in a nursing home.	1	2	3	4	5
I have many conflicts with my parents.	1	2	3	4	5
I can't talk openly with my parents.	1	2	3	4	5
I don't understand my parents.	1	2	3	4	5
My parents interfere with our marriage.	1	2	3	4	5
I'm angry about my parents' divorce.	1	2	3	4	5
I don't want my parent to live with me.	1	2	3	4	5
My parents expect too much of me.	1	2	3	4	5
My parents live their lives through me.	1	2	3	4	5
Other_____	1	2	3	4	5
(list other problem areas)					
_____	1	2	3	4	5

If you circled 3, 4, or 5 for any problem, turn to the workbook section on parents (page 99), where you will find exercises to help you change what you are experiencing.

FRIENDSHIP

Use the following list to identify your problem areas in regard to friendship. After you select statements that fit your circumstances, rate the intensity of each problem by circling a number on the scale from 1 to 5, letting "1" equal a minor problem and "5" equal a major problem.

I can't keep friends.	1	2	3	4	5
I'm afraid of close friendships.	1	2	3	4	5
Friends like me only for my money.	1	2	3	4	5
I can't tell friends my real feelings.	1	2	3	4	5
I frequently feel left out by my friends.	1	2	3	4	5
I'm afraid my friend will reject me.	1	2	3	4	5
I don't know how to make new friends.	1	2	3	4	5
Friends often take advantage of me.	1	2	3	4	5
I am not a very good friend.	1	2	3	4	5
I'm afraid to disagree with friends.	1	2	3	4	5
I'm not as interesting as my friends.	1	2	3	4	5
Friends often let me down.	1	2	3	4	5
I'm afraid to get close to people.	1	2	3	4	5
I can't break away from bad friendships.	1	2	3	4	5
I'm often jealous of my friends.	1	2	3	4	5
I'm afraid my friend will leave me.	1	2	3	4	5
I can't find friends my own age.	1	2	3	4	5
People I want for friends don't like me.	1	2	3	4	5
Other_____	1	2	3	4	5
(list other problem areas)					
_____	1	2	3	4	5

If you circled 3, 4, or 5 for any problem, turn to the workbook section on friendship (page 113), where you will find exercises to help you change what you are experiencing.

GROWING OLDER

Use the following list to identify your problem areas in regard to growing older. After you select statements that fit your circumstances, rate the intensity of each problem by circling a number on the scale from 1 to 5, letting "1" equal a minor problem and "5" equal a major problem.

Growing older scares me.	1	2	3	4	5
I'm not ready for retirement.	1	2	3	4	5
I'll never get remarried at my age.	1	2	3	4	5
I'm afraid of losing my independence.	1	2	3	4	5
I won't have enough money to live on.	1	2	3	4	5
I won't be as sexually capable as I was.	1	2	3	4	5
I'm not as attractive as I used to be.	1	2	3	4	5
I'm afraid of chronic health problems.	1	2	3	4	5
No one will take care of me later on.	1	2	3	4	5
My body doesn't recover like it used to.	1	2	3	4	5
Younger people get all the promotions.	1	2	3	4	5
I'm getting too old to have children.	1	2	3	4	5
My company doesn't want older people.	1	2	3	4	5
I haven't done as much as I wanted to do.	1	2	3	4	5
I worry about providing for my children.	1	2	3	4	5
Growing older depresses me.	1	2	3	4	5
I'm concerned about career advancement.	1	2	3	4	5
I'm afraid younger people won't like me.	1	2	3	4	5
Other_____	1	2	3	4	5

(list other problem areas)

_____	1	2	3	4	5

If you circled 3, 4, or 5 for any problem, turn to the workbook section on growing older (page 127), where you will find exercises to help you change what you are experiencing.

ADDICTION

Use the following list to identify your problem areas in regard to an addiction. After you select statements that fit your circumstances, rate the intensity of each problem by circling a number on the scale from 1 to 5, letting "1" equal a minor problem and "5" equal a major problem.

I can't give up tranquilizers.	1	2	3	4	5
Cocaine rules my life.	1	2	3	4	5
My drinking is out of control.	1	2	3	4	5
I can't control my eating.	1	2	3	4	5
I use TV to escape from life.	1	2	3	4	5
All I eat is junk food.	1	2	3	4	5
I smoke too much pot.	1	2	3	4	5
I can't miss a single soap opera.	1	2	3	4	5
I spend all my time working.	1	2	3	4	5
I can't relax until everything is clean.	1	2	3	4	5
My credit card use is out of control.	1	2	3	4	5
I'm caught up in an abusive relationship.	1	2	3	4	5
I have to have everything perfect.	1	2	3	4	5
I can't control my gambling.	1	2	3	4	5
I never take time to have fun.	1	2	3	4	5
I can't stop smoking.	1	2	3	4	5
I'm compulsive about exercising.	1	2	3	4	5
I can't exist without lots of coffee.	1	2	3	4	5
Other_____	1	2	3	4	5
(list other problem areas)					
_____	1	2	3	4	5

If you circled 3, 4, or 5 for any problem, turn to the workbook section on addiction (page 141), where you will find exercises to help you change what you are experiencing.

SELF-ASSESSMENT

DEATH AND DYING

Use the following list to identify your problem areas in regard to death or dying. After you select statements that fit your circumstances, rate the intensity of each problem by circling a number on the scale from 1 to 5, letting "1" equal a minor problem and "5" equal a major problem.

I am afraid of dying.	1	2	3	4	5
I haven't really lived.	1	2	3	4	5
I worry about what happens after death.	1	2	3	4	5
I still feel guilty about some things.	1	2	3	4	5
I'm afraid of eternal punishment.	1	2	3	4	5
I can't bear the thought of suffering.	1	2	3	4	5
I don't want to leave my family.	1	2	3	4	5
I'll never be able to finish everything.	1	2	3	4	5
I'm worried about medical costs.	1	2	3	4	5
My spouse won't know how to cope.	1	2	3	4	5
I don't want to be a burden to anyone.	1	2	3	4	5
I can't bear to watch my child die.	1	2	3	4	5
I've never really lived.	1	2	3	4	5
I never told my parents I loved them.	1	2	3	4	5
I'm angry that someone I love has died.	1	2	3	4	5
My financial affairs are in a mess.	1	2	3	4	5
I can't go on without my spouse.	1	2	3	4	5
I'm sad that I alienated my children.	1	2	3	4	5

Other_____   1   2   3   4   5
      (list other problem areas)

_____   1   2   3   4   5

If you circled 3, 4, or 5 for any problem, turn to the workbook section on death and dying (page 155), where you will find exercises to help you change what you are experiencing.

EMOTIONAL WELL-BEING

Use the following list to identify your problem areas in regard to emotional well-being. After you select statements that fit your circumstances, rate the intensity of each problem by circling a number on the scale from 1 to 5, letting "1" equal a minor problem and "5" equal a major problem.

I don't have any self-confidence.	1	2	3	4	5
I can't express my feelings.	1	2	3	4	5
I'm very unhappy with life.	1	2	3	4	5
No one understands me.	1	2	3	4	5
I am terribly lonely.	1	2	3	4	5
I can't stop worrying.	1	2	3	4	5
Nobody loves me.	1	2	3	4	5
I get frustrated easily.	1	2	3	4	5
I can't get over past hurts.	1	2	3	4	5
I feel like a failure.	1	2	3	4	5
I am constantly afraid.	1	2	3	4	5
I'm easily intimidated.	1	2	3	4	5
I feel so powerless.	1	2	3	4	5
I get very upset over little things.	1	2	3	4	5
I'm painfully shy.	1	2	3	4	5
I can't control my anger.	1	2	3	4	5
Life seems too heavy at times.	1	2	3	4	5
Other_____	1	2	3	4	5
(list other problem areas)					
_____	1	2	3	4	5

If you circled 3, 4, or 5 for any problem, turn to the workbook section on emotional well-being (page 169), where you will find exercises to help you change what you are experiencing.

SELF-ASSESSMENT

LIFE DIRECTION

Use the following list to identify your problem areas in regard to life direction. After you select statements that fit your circumstances, rate the intensity of each problem by circling a number on the scale from 1 to 5, letting "1" equal a minor problem and "5" equal a major problem.

I feel life is passing me by.	1	2	3	4	5
Nothing I do has much purpose.	1	2	3	4	5
I can't accomplish anything.	1	2	3	4	5
Life isn't fun anymore.	1	2	3	4	5
My life doesn't have meaning.	1	2	3	4	5
I'm very disillusioned with my career.	1	2	3	4	5
All I do is sit home and watch TV.	1	2	3	4	5
I'm not living up to my potential.	1	2	3	4	5
My life never changes.	1	2	3	4	5
I keep changing jobs but nothing helps.	1	2	3	4	5
I feel like a failure.	1	2	3	4	5
I don't know what to do with my life.	1	2	3	4	5
I'm afraid to change.	1	2	3	4	5
I can't find any inspiration.	1	2	3	4	5
I've lost my enthusiasm for life.	1	2	3	4	5
I have nothing new to live for.	1	2	3	4,	5
I never do anything exciting.	1	2	3	4	5
Life is just a daily grind.	1	2	3	4	5
Other_____	1	2	3	4	5
(list other problem areas)					
_____	1	2	3	4	5

If you circled 3, 4, or 5 for any problem, turn to the workbook section on life direction (page 183), where you will find exercises to help you change what you are experiencing.

You Are the One

MONEY

The abundance we desire to experience becomes ours to the degree we rightly accept it as being our experience. The gift of abundance has already been made, but it is up to us to do something about accepting it.

— Ernest Holmes

Give up the idea that you have to struggle for every dollar, that you were "meant" to be poor, or that money worries are just part of life. Free yourself from these limiting beliefs and replace them with the knowledge that everything you need is available to you in infinite supply. Recognize your unity with the Presence and Power of God, and you will attract into your life more abundance than you ever dreamed possible.

When you acquire a new understanding of your unity with the infinite Source of all good, deeply sensing this unity within yourself, money will no longer seem to be withheld from you. It will naturally flow into your life, as the Universal Law of Mind acts upon your personal acceptance of abundance and support.

Money or its equivalent will come to you in many ways. You may receive a present from a friend, an unexpected raise or bonus at work, a reduced price on something you buy, or free tickets to a play. A loan you made but had forgotten about may be suddenly repaid, or you may get an idea for a business that creates fresh avenues of prosperity for you. More important, an ongoing flow of money into your life will be stimulated.

Open yourself to these expressions in your life of the Divine qualities of Abundance and Support. Expect them. Be aware of your unity with God and accept the good you desire. Know that the only limits to the money you can receive and enjoy are those you set for yourself through your beliefs.

The following exercises will help you discover your limiting beliefs and also guide you in using affirmative prayer to resolve any problem you have involving money. Through affirmative prayer you will be lifted into an entirely new understanding of your relationship with money. Remember, don't allow fear to dominate your thinking. Keep in mind always that you are connected with the universal Source of all good.

OLD PATTERNS — NEW POSSIBILITIES

Old Patterns

Your beliefs — which include your thoughts, feelings, and attitudes, both conscious and subconscious — determine what you are now experiencing, for the Universal Law of Mind acts on them to create the circumstances of your life. Use the following exercises to help you become aware of the particular beliefs that underlie your problem with money. Take as much time as you need, perhaps a few days, to respond to these questions since they form an important foundation for the work you will be doing to resolve your problem.

■ Look back at "Where Am I Now?" on the subject of money (page 15). If you haven't completed that exercise, please do so now. Use the space provided below to answer the following questions: What issues did you respond to with a number 3, 4, or 5? Are these issues related? If so, in what way? Select one of them to work with in this section and note it below.

_____

_____

_____

_____

_____

■ Write down the feelings, especially the fears, you have in regard to this issue. What beliefs can you identify about yourself or about other people that underlie these feelings?

_____

_____

_____

_____

_____

_____

■ What new understanding has come to you as a result of exploring these old belief patterns? On the basis of your new understanding, what would you like to change?

_____

_____

_____

_____

_____

_____

_____

_____

_____

New Possibilities

To break up old patterns of thought and behavior, you need to open yourself to new possibilities. The exercise on the following page, based on contrasting statements, will assist you with this process. Saying the statement in the left column first and then saying the statement in the right column will help you become aware of how you think, and also help you break up habitual non-productive patterns of thinking and expand your consciousness. (Create your own statements if the examples provided do not address your situation.)

When you affirm the statements in either the left or the right column, you are directing the activity of the Universal Law of Mind, which creates your experiences according to the patterns of your thoughts, feelings, and attitudes . . . your beliefs. If these beliefs are consistently negative, your experiences will be negative. If these beliefs are positive, your experiences will be positive. Remember, the Universal Law of Mind does not make choices — *you* make the choices through what you believe. *This means you can consciously choose how to direct the Universal Law of Mind to create the results you want.*

You will be working with these consciousness-expanders as a way of preparing for the next section, "Creating My New Life," in which you use affirmative prayer to deal with your specific concern in regard to money. As you read each statement in the right column, see it as a new possibility. Imagine yourself being, acting, and feeling what it expresses. Believe it! Feel the feelings you would have if this statement were actually true right now. In this way you begin the process of changing your thinking.

How do you talk to yourself about your concern? How do you talk to others about it?

If you have been saying:

I don't earn enough money.

I spend too much money.

I have problems borrowing money.

I never have enough money.

I have a poor credit rating.

I have problems getting raises.

I have difficulty saving money.

I'm facing bankruptcy.

I gamble too much.

I can't pay my bills.

I can't buy things I want.

I can't provide for retirement.

I'm afraid of poverty.

I have too many debts.

I'm afraid to let go of money.

I can't pay my taxes.

I'm always worrying about money.

I want large amounts of money.

I don't enjoy the money I have.

I can't manage my money.

Other_____
  (use additional paper if necessary)

Now begin to say:

I earn a great deal of money.

I spend money wisely.

Borrowing money is easy for me.

I always have enough money.

I have a very good credit rating.

I earn raises easily.

I have a savings account.

I am financially successful.

I am free of my need to gamble.

All my bills are paid on time.

I have money to buy what I want.

I am providing for retirement.

I am always financially secure.

I owe very little money.

I joyfully release money.

I have the money to pay taxes.

Everything I need is provided.

I have as much as I can accept.

I love and bless my money.

I manage money well.

_____

Now turn to the next section, "Creating My New Life," to learn to use affirmative prayer to deal with your specific money issue.

DAILY AFFIRMATION:

I have an abundance of money and the universe always supports me.

CREATING MY NEW LIFE

In the previous section you started to see that the Universal Law of Mind acts on your beliefs to create your experiences. You began to identify and break free from negative patterns of belief and you are now aware of new possibilities. *Incorporating any additional understanding you gained in that section, write here what you want your new experience to be.*

_____

_____

_____

_____

This portion of the workbook will help you learn how to create an affirmative prayer to resolve any concern you have in regard to money. In affirmative prayer, you align your thinking with the Divine qualities of Abundance and Support already inherent within you. When you do this, your experience changes. This change occurs as the Universal Law of Mind acts on your new beliefs. (Remember, when we say "beliefs" we mean thoughts, feelings, and attitudes, both conscious and subconscious.)

Realizing through affirmative prayer that Abundance and Support are the truth about God and that you are unified with God, you come to know that abundance and support are also the truth about you in regard to money. As a result, problems are resolved.

Each of the following exercises has two parts. The first part consists of an activity which helps prepare you to write your affirmative prayer. This activity is designed to assist you in developing an inner atmosphere of strong feeling and conviction, one that will make your statements effective. The second part involves actually writing the five stages of your affirmative prayer. Through this process, as you align your thinking with what is true about God, a solution to your money problem unfolds.

Each of the five stages of affirmative prayer — Recognition, Unification, Realization, Thanksgiving, and Release — is explained fully on the following pages: page 70 (Recognition), page 98 (Unification), page 126 (Realization), page 154 (Thanksgiving), and page 182 (Release). Examples are also provided. Be sure to refer to these examples for guidance and suggestions.

1 There is a perfect Presence and Power in the universe. This infinite Life, which expresses as the Divine qualities of Abundance and Support, is the source of all good. Observe these qualities in evidence everywhere: in the vast numbers of stars in the sky and leaves on the trees, in the bountiful rainfall and luxuriant sunshine. Also observe how many different forms of life exist and how lavishly they are provided for. Notice how limitless and bountiful the universe is and how many countless ways abundance is expressed. Recognizing the abiding presence of Divine Abundance and Support, become aware of the activity of God's Power in the world around you. Write in the space below what you think and feel about this Presence and Power.

There is a Presence and Power greater than you are — God — which is the Creator of everything around you. Recognize that there is one God, one Life, one Mind and that it is ever present, ever active, and constantly creative. Now state what you have recognized, letting your statement be as sincere and as meaningful as you can.

(See page 70 for examples of Recognition statements.)

2 As you observe the Presence and Power of God everywhere around you, begin now to experience your deep connection with God. Know you are part of God. Know there is one Life, that Life is God, and that Life is what you are. Know there is one Universal Law of Mind which always responds to your beliefs. Feel your oneness with the Divine qualities of Abundance and Support, taking time to sense the presence of these qualities within you. When has a particular need of yours been completely met? When have you felt a secure sense of being supported and sustained? Remember these occasions and reflect on them. Become still and know that as a spiritual being you are not separate from God-Life, nor are you separate from the Power that gives form to Divine qualities. Write in the space below what this experience of unification feels like.

_____

_____

_____

_____

_____

_____

_____

_____

Observing the Presence and the Power of God everywhere around you, become aware that you are part of a great Unity. Accept and feel your oneness with God. Make a statement below expressing how you experience your oneness with this Presence and Power greater than you are.

_____

_____

_____

_____

_____

(See page 98 for examples of Unification statements.)

3 Maintaining a sense of your unity with a Presence and Power greater than you are, know that Abundance and Support exist in place of your money problem. Contemplate this idea, ridding yourself of all doubt or reservation. Become deeply convinced that the new and positive experience you desire is unfolding for you. Record here the feelings you have as you do this.

Make a positive statement of your changed belief. Write it in the present tense, recognizing and accepting the presence of the Divine qualities of Abundance and Support where your problem appears to be. You are creating a mold for the Universal Law of Mind, so be clear, definite, and specific. Be emphatic! Imagine that what you desire to experience is now established, knowing that it is already taking form in your life through the activity of the Universal Law of Mind. State here what you are now declaring to be true in place of your concern in regard to money.

(See page 126 for examples of Realization statements.)

4 Recall an occasion in your life when you felt a great outpouring of gratitude — whether for something specific or simply for the joy of being alive. Recapture in your imagination this special time of feeling grateful, and allow the experience to be fresh and vivid for you again. Describe here the feelings you have.

When you have an attitude of thanksgiving, knowing your need is already met, something in this attitude enhances your ability to have faith and to be open and receptive. Right now, completely and wholeheartedly accept that your money problem is resolved and feel thankful for this solution. Write a statement here expressing your gratitude.

(See page 154 for examples of Thanksgiving statements.)

5 Have you ever had the experience of feeling completely unburdened, as if a great weight had been lifted from your shoulders? What you felt was a letting go, a release. This is what you need to experience in regard to your money problem. Know that the Universal Law of Mind is now creating the results you desire. Relax and experience a sense of trust, certain that this resolution is unfolding. Write below what the experience of release feels like.

Sometimes you may tend to doubt or deny the good you want to experience. The act of releasing your affirmative prayer helps prevent that. When you release it, the Universal Law of Mind can freely respond to your new spiritual understanding, revealing Abundance and Support in place of your concern. Right now release all fear and worry, and allow this process to move forward. Let go of the problem and be confident that the good you desire is already unfolding. Write a statement releasing your affirmative prayer to the activity of the Universal Law of Mind.

(See page 182 for examples of Release statements.)

MY AFFIRMATIVE PRAYER

Taken together, the statements you have made at the bottom of the previous five pages comprise a complete affirmative prayer, addressing the particular concern about money you have chosen to deal with. This prayer consists of the stages of Recognition, Unification, Realization, Thanksgiving, and Release.

Review each of your five statements now and determine if there are any changes you wish to make in them. As you review them, be sure they evoke deep feeling and conviction in you and are worded concisely for maximum impact. Also be sure they achieve the purpose intended. For example, when you reread your Realization statement, are you able to sense the Abundance and Support of God in your life? After you make any desired changes in your five statements, combine them below into a complete unit.

1 Recognition:

2 Unification:

3 Realization:

4 Thanksgiving:

5 Release:

WHERE DO I GO FROM HERE?

You have now started a process of personal and spiritual growth that will produce new and positive changes for you.

You can do several things to continue the work you started in this section. Stay alert to the statements you make about your situation. At night recall your habitual thought patterns of the day. How much of your thinking was negative and how much was positive? Practice changing the negative statements into positive ones. Say the positive statements over and over until you begin to feel a definite connection with them.

Most important, read your affirmative prayer several times a day. At a minimum, we suggest doing so right before going to bed and upon waking in the morning. Read it out loud if possible. Take time to contemplate it. As you read your prayer and think about it, experience the feelings associated with each of the five stages. Be sure to make reading it meaningful, not simply an automatic exercise. If one of your statements seems to lose impact for you, redo it.

Remain open to change and be willing to follow any inner guidance that comes to you. God works in your life through such inner guidance, which often appears as a new idea or an urge to do something differently. As you allow change to occur, what was originally a problem will be replaced by more desirable circumstances. Remain open-minded and patient, knowing that positive results are certain to take place.

Remember, there is a natural process by which spiritual truth takes form, and the time this process requires varies with different situations. You may have an immediate response to your affirmative prayer, or a period of weeks or even months may elapse, but continue with your affirmative prayer, always using the present tense, accepting that what you desire *is now happening*. Keep deepening your level of conviction and adjust the wording of your prayer to reflect your changed state of consciousness. Feel free to create new affirmations and affirmative prayers as your understanding of your unity with God's Abundance and Support expands. Continue with your affirmative prayer until the desired result is obtained.

HOW AM I CHANGING?

Work with the "Old Patterns — New Possibilities" and "Creating My New Life" sections for two to three weeks, then respond to these questions. They will help you assess your progress and guide you if you need assistance. (Since keeping a record of your experiences is useful when you are seeking to improve your life, you may also want to write your continuing insights in a separate notebook.)

■ What changes have you experienced in your situation as a result of working with this section on money?

_____

_____

_____

■ Are you satisfied with these results? If you are, what do you think is responsible for your improved circumstances?

_____

_____

_____

■ If you feel you are not making progress, go back over the questions and exercises and your responses to them. Do you need to do something differently? Also look at your affirmative prayer. Does it need to be changed? Be sure to check yourself on negative thought habits. Are you willing to reevaluate your approach and try again?

_____

_____

_____

■ What is the most important thing you have learned about yourself in regard to money?

_____

_____

_____

DO YOU RESIST PRAYER?

Affirmative prayer is a practical and effective way to resolve problems, but many people resist using prayer. There are a variety of reasons for this, some of which are noted below. Do any apply to you?

Fear of change. Many of us hesitate to venture into the unknown. We tend to cling to what is familiar in our life, even if we are not happy with it.

Reluctance to give up a problem's hidden benefit or "payoff." For example, we may prefer being unemployed to facing the responsibilities and risks of success.

Diminished expectations. We may become so accustomed to a situation that we don't see the greater possibilities, assuming that not having enough money, feeling stressed, or being lonely is just the way life is.

Low self-esteem. If we don't feel worthy of success, prosperity, health, or love, we tend to deny ourselves the opportunity to experience them.

Desire to appear strong. Taught to take action and be self-reliant, we may view prayer as "giving up." We feel the need to prove that our own efforts are adequate.

Being "lost" without our problem. Whether it involves chronic illness, financial difficulty, strained family relations, or job dissatisfaction, our problem can actually provide us with a sense of who we are. We may fear that if our problem were solved we would lack an identity.

Fear of giving up control. If we have a strong tendency to manage and control the events of our life, we may feel uneasy with the "letting go" and release which prayer involves.

Mistrust of spiritual concepts. We sometimes disregard prayer as a way to solve problems because we haven't learned to use it effectively or we have been taught a limited concept of God.

If you experience resistance due to any of these reasons, know that you can overcome it — and a good way to do so is simply to try using affirmative prayer to deal with a specific problem in your life.

HEALTH

*. . . to the extent we know that God as Life is perfect, whole, and
complete; to the extent that we can mentally accept the Perfection
of the One Life as our life, then to that extent will we be able to enjoy
and experience what previously we may have been lacking — health.*
— Ernest Holmes

Good physical health is basic to joyous, vibrant living. And good health
begins in the mind — with your beliefs, which include your thoughts, feelings, and
attitudes. Positive, life-affirming beliefs result in radiant health, while negative,
pessimistic beliefs tend to cause sickness.

If your thinking has included habitual negative beliefs, you may be experiencing
frequent colds, chronic pain, serious disease, or some other form of illness. But you
don't have to accept these conditions as a way of life. You can enjoy vigorous health
every day of your life — through changing your thinking.

To do this, you need to identify and let go of negative beliefs. (Certain of these
beliefs may even be hidden from your conscious awareness, though they are affect-
ing what happens to your body just as surely as if you were conscious of them.) The
exercises which follow will help you discover any negativity in your thought patterns
and they will also help you refocus your thinking in a more positive direction. Then
as you become aware of the presence of the Wholeness and Vitality of God within
you and align yourself with these Divine qualities, the Universal Law of Mind will
respond by bringing renewed health and vitality into your experience.

Remember that negative beliefs include negative mental and emotional states.
For example, do you feel powerless, angry, out of control, hopeless, depressed,
anxious, or stressed? These attitudes, if persisted in, are almost certain to affect
your body. The exercises in this section suggest a way you can deal with such
negative emotions and also discover any other habits or activities which might be
damaging to your health. (Refer to other workbook sections such as "Emotional
Well-Being" and "Addiction" for additional help.)

Begin now to know that as an expression of the Presence and Power of God you
have a right to vibrant good health. You can control what happens to your body.
You can choose to be healthy. Affirmative prayer opens the way for you to live fully
and live freely — with a radiantly healthy body.

OLD PATTERNS — NEW POSSIBILITIES

Old Patterns

Your beliefs — which include your thoughts, feelings, and attitudes, both conscious and subconscious — determine what you are now experiencing, for the Universal Law of Mind acts on them to create the circumstances of your life. Use the following exercises to help you become aware of the particular beliefs that underlie your health problem. Take as much time as you need, perhaps a few days, to respond to these questions since they form an important foundation for the work you will be doing to resolve your problem.

■ Look back at "Where Am I Now?" on the subject of health (page 16). If you haven't completed that exercise, please do so now. Use the space provided below to answer the following questions: What issues did you respond to with a number 3, 4, or 5? Are these issues related? If so, in what way? Select one of them to work with in this section and note it below.

_____

_____

_____

_____

_____

_____

_____

■ Write down the feelings, especially the fears, you have in regard to this issue. What beliefs can you identify about yourself or about other people that underlie these feelings?

_____

_____

_____

_____

_____

_____

_____

■ What new understanding has come to you as a result of exploring these old belief patterns? On the basis of your new understanding, what would you like to change?

_____

_____

_____

_____

_____

_____

_____

_____

New Possibilities

To break up old patterns of thought and behavior, you need to open yourself to new possibilities. The exercise on the following page, based on contrasting statements, will assist you with this process. Saying the statement in the left column first and then saying the statement in the right column will help you become aware of how you think, and also help you break up habitual non-productive patterns of thinking and expand your consciousness. (Create your own statements if the examples provided do not address your situation.)

When you affirm the statements in either the left or the right column, you are directing the activity of the Universal Law of Mind, which creates your experiences according to the patterns of your thoughts, feelings, and attitudes . . . your beliefs. If these beliefs are consistently negative, your experiences will be negative. If these beliefs are positive, your experiences will be positive. Remember, the Universal Law of Mind does not make choices — _you_ make the choices through what you believe. _This means you can consciously choose how to direct the Universal Law of Mind to create the results you want._

You will be working with these consciousness-expanders as a way of preparing for the next section, "Creating My New Life," in which you use affirmative prayer to deal with your specific health concern. As you read each statement in the right column, see it as a new possibility. Imagine yourself being, acting, and feeling what it expresses. Believe it! Feel the feelings you would have if this statement were actually true right now. In this way you begin the process of changing your thinking.

How do you talk to yourself about your problem? How do you talk to others about it?

If you have been saying:

I always get colds or the flu.

I can't control my weight.

I don't have any energy.

I can't sleep at night.

I worry about recovering from surgery.

I'm afraid of heart trouble.

I suffer from a lot of allergies.

I am in constant pain.

I am dying.

I have a bad back.

I can't function sexually as I want to.

I don't heal quickly.

Everyone in my family gets ulcers.

I can hardly move because of arthritis.

High blood pressure runs in my family.

It's hard for me to breathe at times.

My body feels like it's very old.

I have cancer.

I've always been heavy.

I'll never be very healthy.

Other_____

  (use additional paper if necessary)

Now begin to say:

I am free of colds or the flu.

I maintain my ideal weight.

My body feels alive and energetic.

I sleep deeply and peacefully all night.

I make a complete recovery from surgery.

I have a strong heart.

I am clear of allergies.

I am free from pain.

I accept total healing now.

My back is strong and flexible.

My sexual functioning is excellent.

I heal quickly.

I have a healthy digestive system.

My body moves with ease.

I am free of high blood pressure.

I breathe easily and fully.

My body feels young and healthy.

I am free of cancer.

My past is not my present.

I enjoy full, robust health.

_____

Now turn to the next section, "Creating My New Life," to learn to use affirmative prayer to deal with your specific issue relating to health.

DAILY AFFIRMATION:

I accept wholeness and vitality as the truth about my body.

CREATING MY NEW LIFE

In the previous section you started to see that the Universal Law of Mind acts on your beliefs to create your experiences. You began to identify and break free from negative patterns of belief and you are now aware of new possibilities. *Incorporating any additional understanding you gained in that section, write here what you want your new experience to be.*

This portion of the workbook will help you learn how to create an affirmative prayer to resolve the concern you have in regard to health. In affirmative prayer, you align your thinking with the Divine qualities of Wholeness and Vitality already inherent within you. When you do this, your experience changes. This change occurs as the Universal Law of Mind acts on your new beliefs. (Remember, when we say "beliefs" we mean thoughts, feelings, and attitudes, both conscious and subconscious.)

Realizing through affirmative prayer that Wholeness and Vitality are the truth about God and that you are unified with God, you come to know that wholeness and vitality are also the truth about you in regard to health. As a result, problems are resolved.

Each of the following exercises has two parts. The first part consists of an activity which helps prepare you to write your affirmative prayer. This activity is designed to assist you in developing an inner atmosphere of strong feeling and conviction, one that will make your statements effective. The second part involves actually writing the five stages of your affirmative prayer. Through this process, as you align your thinking with what is true about God, a solution to your health problem unfolds.

Each of the five stages of affirmative prayer — Recognition, Unification, Realization, Thanksgiving, and Release — is explained fully on the following pages: page 70 (Recognition), page 98 (Unification), page 126 (Realization), page 154 (Thanksgiving), and page 182 (Release). Examples are also provided. Be sure to refer to these examples for guidance and suggestions.

1 The perfect Presence and Power of God exists everywhere and expresses as Wholeness and Vitality. Notice evidence of these Divine qualities in the world around you, whether as a plant flourishing on the window sill or as lush vegetation covering parks, lawns, or hillsides. Recognizing this evidence of the abiding presence of Divine Wholeness and Vitality, become aware of the activity of God's Power in the world around you. Write in the space below what you think and feel about this Presence and Power.

There is a Presence and Power greater than you are — God — which is the Creator of everything around you. Recognize that there is one God, one Life, one Mind and that it is ever present, ever active, and constantly creative. Now state what you have recognized, letting your statement be as sincere and meaningful as you can.

(See page 70 for examples of Recognition statements.)

2 As you observe the Presence and Power of God everywhere around you, begin now to experience your deep connection with God. Know there is one Life, that Life is God, and that Life is what you are. Know there is one Universal Law of Mind which always responds to your beliefs. Feel your oneness with the Divine qualities of Wholeness and Vitality, taking time to sense the presence of these qualities within you. When have you felt particularly energetic and alive? When have you observed in your body the mending of a broken bone or the healing of a cut? Remember these occasions and reflect on them. Become still and know that as a spiritual being you are not separate from God-Life, nor are you separate from the Power that gives form to Divine qualities. Write in the space below what this experience of unification feels like.

_____

_____

_____

_____

_____

_____

_____

_____

_____

Observing the Presence and the Power of God everywhere around you, become aware that you are part of a great Unity. Accept and feel your oneness with God. Make a statement below expressing how you experience your oneness with this Presence and Power greater than you are.

_____

_____

_____

_____

_____

(See page 98 for examples of Unification statements.)

3 Maintaining a sense of your unity with a Presence and Power greater than you are, know that Wholeness and Vitality exist in place of your concern about health. Contemplate this idea, ridding yourself of all doubt or reservation. Become deeply convinced that the new and positive experience you desire is unfolding for you. Record here the feelings you have as you do this.

_____

_____

_____

_____

_____

_____

_____

_____

_____

_____

Make a positive statement of your changed belief. Write it in the present tense, recognizing and accepting the presence of the Divine qualities of Wholeness and Vitality where your problem appears to be. You are creating a mold for the Universal Law of Mind, so be clear, definite, and specific. Be emphatic! Imagine that what you desire to experience is now established, knowing that it is already taking form in your life through the activity of the Universal Law of Mind. State here what you are now declaring to be true in place of your concern about health.

_____

_____

_____

_____

(See page 126 for examples of Realization statements.)

4 Recall an occasion in your life when you felt a great outpouring of gratitude — whether for something specific or simply for the joy of being alive. Recapture in your imagination this special time of feeling grateful, and allow the experience to be fresh and vivid for you again. Describe here the feelings you have.

When you have an attitude of thanksgiving, knowing your need is already met, something in this attitude enhances your ability to have faith and to be open and receptive. Right now, completely and wholeheartedly accept that your health concern is resolved and feel thankful for this solution. Write a statement here expressing your gratitude.

(See page 154 for examples of Thanksgiving statements.)

5 Have you ever had the experience of feeling completely unburdened, as if a great weight had been lifted from your shoulders? What you felt was a letting go, a release. This is what you need to experience in regard to your health problem. Know that the Universal Law of Mind is creating the results you desire. Relax and experience a sense of trust, certain that this resolution is now unfolding. Write below what the experience of release feels like.

Sometimes you may tend to doubt or deny the good you want to experience. The act of releasing your affirmative prayer helps prevent that. When you release it, the Universal Law of Mind can freely respond to your new spiritual understanding, revealing Wholeness and Vitality in place of your concern. Right now release all fear and worry, and allow this process to move forward. Let go of the problem and be confident that the good you desire is already unfolding. Write a statement releasing your affirmative prayer to the activity of the Universal Law of Mind.

(See page 182 for examples of Release statements.)

MY AFFIRMATIVE PRAYER

Taken together, the statements you have made at the bottom of the previous five pages comprise a complete affirmative prayer, addressing the particular concern about health you have chosen to deal with. This prayer consists of the stages of Recognition, Unification, Realization, Thanksgiving, and Release.

Review each of your five statements now and determine if there are any changes you wish to make in them. As you review them, be sure they evoke deep feeling and conviction in you and are worded concisely for maximum impact. Also be sure they achieve the purpose intended. For example, when you reread your Realization statement, are you able to sense the Vitality and Wholeness of God in your life? After you make any desired changes in your five statements, combine them below into a complete unit.

1 Recognition: _____

_____

_____

2 Unification: _____

_____

_____

3 Realization: _____

_____

_____

4 Thanksgiving: _____

_____

_____

5 Release: _____

_____

_____

WHERE DO I GO FROM HERE?

You have now started a process of personal and spiritual growth that will produce new and positive changes for you.

You can do several things to continue the work you started in this section. Stay alert to the statements you make about your situation. At night recall your habitual thought patterns of the day. How much of your thinking was negative and how much was positive? Practice changing the negative statements into positive ones. Say the positive statements over and over until you begin to feel a definite connection with them.

Most important, read your affirmative prayer several times a day. At a minimum, we suggest doing so right before going to bed and upon waking in the morning. Read it out loud if possible. Take time to contemplate it. As you read your prayer and think about it, experience the feelings associated with each of the five stages. Be sure to make reading it meaningful, not simply an automatic exercise. If one of your statements seems to lose impact for you, redo it.

Remain open to change and be willing to follow any inner guidance that comes to you. God works in your life through such inner guidance, which often appears as a new idea or an urge to do something differently. As you allow change to occur, what was originally a problem will be replaced by more desirable circumstances. Remain open-minded and patient, knowing that positive results are certain to take place.

Remember, there is a natural process by which spiritual truth takes form, and the time this process requires varies with different situations. You may have an immediate response to your affirmative prayer, or a period of weeks or even months may elapse, but continue with your affirmative prayer, always using the present tense, accepting that what you desire *is now happening*. Keep deepening your level of conviction and adjust the wording of your prayer to reflect your changed state of consciousness. Feel free to create new affirmations and affirmative prayers as your understanding of your unity with God's Vitality and Wholeness expands. Continue with your affirmative prayer until the desired result is obtained.

HOW AM I CHANGING?

Work with the "Old Patterns — New Possibilities" and "Creating My New Life" sections for two to three weeks, then respond to these questions. They will help you assess your progress and guide you if you need assistance. (Since keeping a record of your experiences is useful when you are seeking to improve your life, you may also want to write your continuing insights in a separate notebook.)

■ What changes have you experienced in your situation as a result of working with this section on health?

_____

_____

_____

■ Are you satisfied with these results? If you are, what do you think is responsible for your improved circumstances?

_____

_____

_____

■ If you feel you are not making progress, go back over the questions and exercises and your responses to them. Do you need to do something differently? Also look at your affirmative prayer. Does it need to be changed? Be sure to check yourself on negative thought habits. Are you willing to reevaluate your approach and try again?

_____

_____

_____

■ What is the most important thing you have learned about yourself in regard to health?

_____

_____

_____

EMPLOYMENT

I know that I am in partnership with the Infinite. I identify myself with this partnership knowing that it always leads to success. I accept that the action of infinite Intelligence is back of everything. It is always manifesting Itself and It now does so through the thought pattern of success I am establishing for myself. — Ernest Holmes

Because your essential nature is spiritual, you are endowed with unlimited energy, intelligence, talent, and creativity. You have also been given an inner urge to express these aspects of your nature, and one way of expressing them is through the work you do.

Success in work or business is both personally fulfilling and financially rewarding, but occasionally problems occur. For example, you may be having difficulty finding a job or getting the promotion you want, you may be facing conflict or discrimination on the job, or your business may not be bringing in the income you desire. If one of these problems confronts you, know that you can resolve it through affirmative prayer.

Whatever you are now experiencing in the area of employment or business is the result of your beliefs — your thoughts, feelings, and attitudes. The Universal Law of Mind acts upon these beliefs to create corresponding life experiences. Thus, negative beliefs — such as "I can't find a good job" or "I'll never get ahead in business" — lead to negative experiences. To enjoy new, positive experiences, you need new, positive beliefs.

Begin by knowing right now that you can find the financially rewarding and challenging work you want. Feel worthy of a promotion or a raise. Know that you are in control of what you experience in your job or business. Explore your beliefs and eliminate any that are not productive, replacing them with the firm conviction that right now you are successful and fulfilled.

Remember, you are never alone. Always you have within you the Presence and Power of God, your Silent Partner. Through affirmative prayer you can bring into expression in your life the Success and Fulfillment ever available from this Divine Source.

OLD PATTERNS — NEW POSSIBILITIES

Old Patterns

Your beliefs — which include your thoughts, feelings, and attitudes, both conscious and subconscious — determine what you are now experiencing, for the Universal Law of Mind acts on them to create the circumstances of your life. Use the following exercises to help you become aware of the particular beliefs that underlie your concern about employment. Take as much time as you need, perhaps a few days, to respond to these questions since they form an important foundation for helping you resolve your problem.

■ Look back at "Where Am I Now?" on the subject of employment (page 17). If you haven't completed that exercise, please do so now. Use the space provided below to answer the following questions: What issues did you respond to with a number 3, 4, or 5? Are these issues related? If so, in what way? Select one of them to work with in this section and note it below.

_____

_____

_____

_____

_____

_____

■ Write down the feelings, especially the fears, you have in regard to this issue. What beliefs can you identify about yourself or about other people that underlie these feelings?

_____

_____

_____

_____

_____

_____

■ What new understanding has come to you as a result of exploring these old belief patterns? On the basis of your new understanding, what would you like to change?

_____

_____

_____

_____

_____

_____

_____

_____

New Possibilities

To break up old patterns of thought and behavior, you need to open yourself to new possibilities. The exercise on the following page, based on contrasting statements, will assist you with this process. Saying the statement in the left column first and then saying the statement in the right column will help you become aware of how you think, and also help you break up habitual non-productive patterns of thinking and expand your consciousness. (Create your own statements if the examples provided do not address your situation.)

When you affirm the statements in either the left or the right column, you are directing the activity of the Universal Law of Mind, which creates your experiences according to the patterns of your thoughts, feelings, and attitudes . . . your beliefs. If these beliefs are consistently negative, your experiences will be negative. If these beliefs are positive, your experiences will be positive. Remember, the Universal Law of Mind does not make choices — *you* make the choices through what you believe. *This means you can consciously choose how to direct the Universal Law of Mind to create the results you want.*

You will be working with these consciousness-expanders as a way of preparing for the next section, "Creating My New Life," in which you use affirmative prayer to deal with your specific concern regarding employment. As you read each statement in the right column, see it as a new possibility. Imagine yourself being, acting, and feeling what it expresses. Believe it! Feel the feelings you would have if this statement were actually true right now. In this way you begin the process of changing your thinking.

How do you talk to yourself about your problem? How do you talk to others about it?

If you have been saying:	Now begin to say:
I'm overstressed on my job.	I pace myself and am relaxed.
I'll never get the promotion I deserve.	I have the promotion I wanted.
I don't know where to go with my career.	I am focused and have new career goals.
I can't be creative on my job.	My job provides creative outlets.
I can't hold a job.	I am a valued employee.
I'm afraid of job interviews.	I do very well in job interviews.
I don't get along with my coworkers.	I enjoy being with my coworkers.
The competition is ruining my business.	There is plenty for everyone.
I don't have any job prospects.	I have several job offers.
I can't get competent help.	I have highly qualified employees.
I'll never be a success.	I am as successful as I want to be.
I have difficulty firing people.	I release people with dignity.
I'm afraid to supervise people.	I am a competent supervisor.
I'm discriminated against on the job.	I'm totally accepted at work.
My job doesn't pay enough.	I am highly paid.
My boss doesn't appreciate me.	I am appreciated by my boss.
I have a hard time working and being a mother.	I have a good support system to help me.
My job is too far from home.	I have a job close to home.
I'm sexually harassed at work.	I am treated with respect on my job.
My business is failing.	My business is prospering.

Other_____   _____
   (use additional paper if necessary)

Now turn to the next section, "Creating My New Life," to learn to use affirmative prayer to deal with your specific issue relating to employment.

DAILY AFFIRMATION:

I am successful and fulfilled in the work I do.

CREATING MY NEW LIFE

In the previous section you started to see that the Universal Law of Mind acts on your beliefs to create your experiences. You began to identify and break free from negative patterns of belief and you are now aware of new possibilities. *Incorporating any additional understanding you gained in that section, write here what you want your new experience to be.*

_____

_____

_____

_____

This portion of the workbook will help you learn how to create an affirmative prayer to resolve any concern you have in regard to employment. In affirmative prayer, you align your thinking with the Divine qualities of Success and Fulfillment already inherent within you. When you do this, your experience changes. This change occurs as the Universal Law of Mind acts on your new beliefs. (Remember, when we say "beliefs" we mean thoughts, feelings, and attitudes, both conscious and subconscious.)

Realizing through affirmative prayer that Success and Fulfillment are the truth about God and that you are unified with God, you come to know that success and fulfillment are also the truth about you in regard to employment. As a result, problems are resolved.

Each of the following exercises has two parts. The first part consists of an activity which helps prepare you to write your affirmative prayer. This activity is designed to assist you in developing an inner atmosphere of strong feeling and conviction, one that will make your statements effective. The second part involves actually writing the five stages of your affirmative prayer. Through this process, as you align your thinking with what is true about God, a solution to your employment problem unfolds.

Each of the five stages of affirmative prayer — Recognition, Unification, Realization, Thanksgiving, and Release — is explained fully on the following pages: page 70 (Recognition), page 98 (Unification), page 126 (Realization), page 154 (Thanksgiving), and page 182 (Release). Examples are also provided. Be sure to refer to these examples for guidance and suggestions.

1 The perfect Presence and Power of God exists everywhere and expresses as Success and Fulfillment. These Divine qualities are especially evident in nature. Notice, for example, the innate drive of plants and animals to succeed in adapting to their environment. Also notice the unceasing urge within all of life to express in the fullest and most complete way possible. Recognizing evidence of the Divine qualities of Success and Fulfillment, become aware of the activity of God's Power in the world around you. Write in the space below what you think and feel about this Presence and Power.

There is a Presence and Power greater than you are — God — which is the Creator of everything around you. Recognize that there is one God, one Life, one Mind and that it is ever present, ever active, and constantly creative. Now state what you have recognized, letting your statement be as sincere and as meaningful as you can.

(See page 70 for examples of Recognition statements.)

2 As you observe the Presence and Power of God everywhere around you, begin now to experience your deep connection with God. Know you are part of God. Know there is one Life, that Life is God, and that Life is what you are. Know there is one Universal Law of Mind which always responds to your beliefs. Feel your oneness with the Divine qualities of Success and Fulfillment, taking time to sense the presence of these qualities within you. Think of times when you met with great success and felt deeply fulfilled. Remember these occasions and reflect on them. Become still and know that as a spiritual being you are not separate from God-Life, nor are you separate from the Power that gives form to Divine qualities. Write in the space below what this experience of unification feels like.

Observing the Presence and the Power of God everywhere around you, become aware that you are part of a great Unity. Accept and feel your oneness with God. Make a statement below expressing how you experience your oneness with this Presence and Power greater than you are.

(See page 98 for examples of Unification statements.)

3 Maintaining a sense of your unity with a Presence and Power greater than you are, know that Success and Fulfillment exist in place of your employment problem. Contemplate this idea, ridding yourself of all doubt or reservation. Become deeply convinced that the new and positive experience you desire is unfolding for you. Record here the feelings you have as you do this.

Make a positive statement of your changed belief. Write it in the present tense, recognizing and accepting the presence of the Divine qualities of Success and Fulfillment where your problem appears to be. You are creating a mold for the Universal Law of Mind, so be clear, definite, and specific. Be emphatic! Imagine that what you desire to experience is now established, knowing that it is already taking form in your life through the activity of the Universal Law of Mind. State here what you are now declaring to be true in place of your problem.

(See page 126 for examples of Realization statements.)

4 Recall an occasion in your life when you felt a great outpouring of gratitude — whether for something specific or simply for the joy of being alive. Recapture in your imagination this special time of feeling grateful, and allow the experience to be fresh and vivid for you again. Describe here the feelings you have.

When you have an attitude of thanksgiving, knowing your need is already met, something in this attitude enhances your ability to have faith and to be open and receptive. Right now, completely and wholeheartedly accept that your employment concern is resolved and feel thankful for this solution. Write a statement here expressing your gratitude.

(See page 154 for examples of Thanksgiving statements.)

5 Have you ever had the experience of feeling completely unburdened, as if a great weight had been lifted from your shoulders? What you felt was a letting go, a release. This is what you need to experience in regard to your employment or business problem. Know that the Universal Law of Mind is now creating what you desire. Relax and know, with a sense of trust, that this resolution is unfolding. Write below what the experience of release feels like.

_____

_____

_____

_____

_____

_____

_____

_____

_____

Sometimes you may tend to doubt or deny the good you want to experience. The act of releasing your affirmative prayer helps prevent that. When you release it, the Universal Law of Mind can freely respond to your new spiritual understanding, revealing Success and Fulfillment in place of your concern. Right now release all fear and worry, and allow this process to move forward. Let go of the problem and be confident that the good you desire is already unfolding. Write a statement releasing your affirmative prayer to the activity of the Universal Law of Mind.

_____

_____

_____

_____

(See page 182 for examples of Release statements.)

MY AFFIRMATIVE PRAYER

Taken together, the statements you have made at the bottom of the previous five pages comprise a complete affirmative prayer, addressing the particular concern about employment you have chosen to deal with. This prayer consists of the stages of Recognition, Unification, Realization, Thanksgiving, and Release.

Review each of your five statements now and determine if there are any changes you wish to make in them. As you review them, be sure they evoke deep feeling and conviction in you and are worded concisely for maximum impact. Also be sure they achieve the purpose intended. For example, when you reread your Realization statement, are you able to sense the Success and Fulfillment of God in your life? After you make any desired changes in your five statements, combine them below into a complete unit.

1 Recognition:

2 Unification:

3 Realization:

4 Thanksgiving:

5 Release:

WHERE DO I GO FROM HERE?

You have now started a process of personal and spiritual growth that will produce new and positive changes for you.

You can do several things to continue the work you started in this section. Stay alert to the statements you make about your situation. At night recall your habitual thought patterns of the day. How much of your thinking was negative and how much was positive? Practice changing the negative statements into positive ones. Say the positive statements over and over until you begin to feel a definite connection with them.

Most important, read your affirmative prayer several times a day. At a minimum, we suggest doing so right before going to bed and upon waking in the morning. Read it out loud if possible. Take time to contemplate it. As you read your prayer and think about it, experience the feelings associated with each of the five stages. Be sure to make reading it meaningful, not simply an automatic exercise. If one of your statements seems to lose impact for you, redo it.

Remain open to change and be willing to follow any inner guidance that comes to you. God works in your life through such inner guidance, which often appears as a new idea or an urge to do something differently. As you allow change to occur, what was originally a problem will be replaced by more desirable circumstances. Remain open-minded and patient, knowing that positive results are certain to take place.

Remember, there is a natural process by which spiritual truth takes form, and the time this process requires varies with different situations. You may have an immediate response to your affirmative prayer, or a period of weeks or even months may elapse, but continue with your affirmative prayer, always using the present tense, accepting that what you desire *is now happening*. Keep deepening your level of conviction and adjust the wording of your prayer to reflect your changed state of consciousness. Feel free to create new affirmations and affirmative prayers as your understanding of your unity with God's Success and Fulfillment expands. Continue with your affirmative prayer until the desired result is obtained.

HOW AM I CHANGING?

Work with the "Old Patterns — New Possibilities" and "Creating My New Life" sections for two to three weeks, then respond to these questions. They will help you assess your progress and guide you if you need assistance. (Since keeping a record of your experiences is useful when you are seeking to improve your life, you may also want to write your continuing insights in a separate notebook.)

■ What changes have you experienced in your situation as a result of working with this section on employment?

_____

_____

_____

_____

■ Are you satisfied with these results? If you are, what do you think is responsible for your improved circumstances?

_____

_____

_____

_____

■ If you feel you are not making progress, go back over the questions and exercises and your responses to them. Do you need to do something differently? Also look at your affirmative prayer. Does it need to be changed? Be sure to check yourself on negative thought habits. Are you willing to reevaluate your approach and try again?

_____

_____

_____

_____

■ What is the most important thing you have learned about yourself in regard to business or employment?

_____

_____

_____

_____

RECOGNITION

Recognition is the first stage of affirmative prayer. In this stage you recognize God as the ultimate Presence and Power in the universe. There is only God. God *is* everything, and God is *in* everything.

Purpose of the Recognition stage of affirmative prayer: To create within yourself a greater awareness of the existence of God; to expand your understanding of the nature of God as the Source and Creator of everything in life.

Suggestions for creating an effective statement of recognition: A recognition statement reflects the depth of your conviction that there is a Presence and Power in the universe greater than you are that is Life itself. In preparing to make your statement, become quiet and contemplate what this Divine Presence and Power — God — means to you. During this period sort through your beliefs about God. Then begin to think of the qualities of God you are most familiar with. Choose a quality to contemplate and explore the significance it has for you. (From the sections in this workbook, you might select one of the qualities of God related to the problem area you are working on.) Let your thoughts roam freely as you reflect on this quality so you can arrive at a much greater concept than you had before. Then, turning your thoughts toward God, contemplate God as the Source of this quality and of all other good that you experience.

Spend as much time as you need reflecting on this quality and when you feel you have reached a deeper level of recognition of God as the Presence and Power in and through everything, put words to your thoughts and make a statement that expresses what you recognize about God. Record your statement on the appropriate page of this workbook.

Examples of Recognition statements:

☐ I know there is a Presence and Power in the universe that is the source of all life. This Presence radiates in and through everything and it is personal to me right now.

☐ There is a Power for good in the universe greater than I am, which I call God. I am always surrounded by this Power, which intelligently responds to me. It is in me and also in everything.

☐ I am aware at the deepest level of my being that there is only God expressing in and as everything in the universe. I recognize the Goodness of God, the Peace of God, and the Love of God in all life.

MARRIAGE

What a difference it would make in our human relationships if we tried to sense the full meaning of the Divine incarnation in all people and adjusted our viewpoint to the truth that we are all bound together in the unity of God.
— Ernest Holmes

Marriage, or any intimate primary relationship, joins two people in a unique experience of loving and caring for each other, of sharing hopes and fears, of working and cooperating toward common goals, and of meeting the challenges of life together.

A journey of great richness, marriage offers a life filled with excitement and joy. But there are many ways in which marriage can also involve conflict and frustration. How do you deal with the difficult times? What do you do when the bonds of love and closeness seem to weaken and you feel all alone, when you and your partner clash on an important issue, when you lose a sense of being an individual with your own identity, or when you feel bored and stifled? Or, if you are not presently in a relationship but want to be, how do you find a partner who is right for you?

By changing your beliefs, you can solve these and any other problem relating to marriage and primary relationships. When you use affirmative prayer, recognizing your unity with the Presence and Power of God, you allow the Divine qualities of Love and Harmony to be more fully expressed in your experience. A loving and harmonious situation naturally unfolds for you, as the Universal Law of Mind responds to your positive new beliefs.

Through affirmative prayer, you recognize that the perfect Life of God is expressing in your relationship and that neither you nor your partner is ever separate from the Love and Harmony that flow from this infinite Source. Begin now to explore the beliefs that underlie what you are presently experiencing, replacing negative beliefs with positive beliefs that affirm spiritual truths. In this way, you redirect the activity of the Universal Law of Mind, which then brings forth the joyous, fulfilling, and happy relationship you desire.

OLD PATTERNS — NEW POSSIBILITIES

Old Patterns

Your beliefs — which include your thoughts, feelings, and attitudes, both conscious and subconscious — determine what you are now experiencing, for the Universal Law of Mind acts on them to create the circumstances of your life. Use the following exercises to help you become aware of the particular beliefs that underlie your concern in regard to marriage. Take as much time as you need, perhaps a few days, to respond to these questions since they form an important foundation for the work you will be doing to resolve your concern.

■ Look back at "Where Am I Now?" on the subject of marriage (page 18). If you haven't completed that exercise, please do so now. Use the space provided below to answer the following questions: What issues did you respond to with a number 3, 4, or 5? Are these issues related? If so, in what way? Select one of them to work with in this section and note it below.

_____

_____

_____

_____

_____

_____

■ Write down the feelings, especially the fears, you have in regard to this issue. What beliefs can you identify about yourself or about other people that underlie these feelings?

_____

_____

_____

_____

_____

■ What new understanding has come to you as a result of exploring these old belief patterns? On the basis of your new understanding, what would you like to change?

_____

_____

_____

_____

_____

_____

_____

_____

New Possibilities

To break up old patterns of thought and behavior, you need to open yourself to new possibilities. The exercise on the following page, based on contrasting statements, will assist you with this process. Saying the statement in the left column first and then saying the statement in the right column will help you become aware of how you think, and also help you break up habitual non-productive patterns of thinking and expand your consciousness. (Create your own statements if the examples provided do not address your situation.)

When you affirm the statements in either the left or the right column, you are directing the activity of the Universal Law of Mind, which creates your experiences according to the patterns of your thoughts, feelings, and attitudes . . . your beliefs. If these beliefs are consistently negative, your experiences will be negative. If these beliefs are positive, your experiences will be positive. Remember, the Universal Law of Mind does not make choices — *you* make the choices through what you believe. *This means you can consciously choose how to direct the Universal Law of Mind to create the results you want.*

You will be working with these consciousness-expanders as a way of preparing for the next section, "Creating My New Life," in which you use affirmative prayer to deal with your concern in regard to marriage. As you read each statement in the right column, see it as a new possibility. Imagine yourself being, acting, and feeling what it expresses. Believe it! Feel the feelings you would have if this statement were actually true right now. In this way you begin the process of changing your thinking.

How do you talk to yourself about your concern? How do you talk to others about it?

If you have been saying:	Now begin to say:
I'm bored with this relationship.	I find new joy in this relationship.
Our sex life is routine and unfulfilling.	We have an exciting sex life.
I can never do what I want to do.	I accept responsibility for myself.
My partner doesn't appreciate me.	I always feel appreciated.
We can't talk about our problems.	We talk openly about any problem.
We have problems with intimacy.	We discover new ways to be close.
I don't feel loved.	I feel very loved.
We fight all the time.	We lovingly express differences.
I want to find a loving partner.	I have the perfect partner.
We don't like each other's friends.	We respect each other's friendships.
We disagree about how to spend money.	We talk frankly about our differences.
My partner abuses me.	I no longer let myself be abused.
We can't agree on how to have fun.	We discover new ways to have fun.
I want to get married.	I am married to my perfect mate.
We have conflicts over religion.	We respect each other's religious beliefs.
I dislike my partner's routines.	I affirm my partner's individuality.
We don't agree on childraising.	We resolve our differences.
My partner makes all the decisions.	I share responsibility for decisions.
My partner has irritating habits.	I release my irritation.
My in-laws are always interfering.	I lovingly set boundaries.

Other_____   _____
   (use additional paper if necessary)

Now turn to the next section, "Creating My New Life," to learn to use affirmative prayer to deal with your specific problem in regard to marriage or a primary relationship.

DAILY AFFIRMATION:

I accept harmony and love in our relationship.

CREATING MY NEW LIFE

In the previous section you started to see that the Universal Law of Mind acts on your beliefs to create your experiences. You began to identify and break free from negative patterns of belief and you are now aware of new possibilities. *Incorporating any additional understanding you gained in that section, write here what you want your new experience to be.*

_____

_____

_____

_____

This portion of the workbook will help you learn how to create an affirmative prayer to resolve your concern with regard to marriage. In affirmative prayer, you align your thinking with the Divine qualities of Love and Harmony already inherent within you. When you do this, your experience changes. This change occurs as the Universal Law of Mind acts on your new beliefs. (Remember, when we say "beliefs" we mean thoughts, feelings, and attitudes, both conscious and subconscious.)

Realizing through affirmative prayer that Love and Harmony are the truth about God and that you are unified with God, you come to know that love and harmony are also the truth about you in regard to your marriage or relationship. As a result, problems are resolved.

Each of the following exercises has two parts. The first part consists of an activity which helps prepare you to write your affirmative prayer. This activity is designed to assist you in developing an inner atmosphere of strong feeling and conviction, one that will make your statements effective. The second part involves actually writing the five stages of your affirmative prayer. Through this process, as you align your thinking with what is true about God, a solution to your concern about marriage unfolds.

Each of the five stages of affirmative prayer — Recognition, Unification, Realization, Thanksgiving, and Release — is explained fully on the following pages: page 70 (Recognition), page 98 (Unification), page 126 (Realization), page 154 (Thanksgiving), and page 182 (Release). Examples are also provided. Be sure to refer to these examples for guidance and suggestions.

1 The perfect Presence and Power of God exists everywhere and expresses as Love and Harmony. Observe the rich and varied evidence of these Divine qualities in the world around you: the givingness of the universe in providing sunshine and rainfall, the loving look in the eyes of someone dear to you, a caring touch, the rhythm of the seasons, the cosmic order of the planets and galaxies. Recognizing the qualities of Love and Harmony everywhere, become aware of the activity of God's Power in the world around you. Write in the space below what you think and feel about this Presence and Power.

There is a Presence and Power greater than you are — God — which is the Source and the Creator of everything around you. Recognize that there is one God, one Life, one Mind and that it is ever present, ever active, and constantly creative. Now state what you have recognized, letting your statement be as sincere and meaningful as you can.

(See page 70 for examples of Recognition statements.)

2 As you observe the Presence and Power of God everywhere around you, begin to experience your deep connection with God. Know you are part of God. Know there is one Life, that Life is God, and that Life is what you are. Know there is one Universal Law of Mind which always responds to your beliefs. Feel your oneness with the Divine qualities of Love and Harmony, taking time to sense the presence of these qualities within you. Think of a time when you felt particularly loving or when you sensed yourself in harmony with the rest of the world. Remember these occasions and reflect on them. Become still and know that as a spiritual being you are not separate from God-Life, nor are you separate from the Power that gives form to Divine qualities. Write in the space below what this experience of unification feels like.

Observing the Presence and the Power of God everywhere around you, become aware that you are part of a great Unity. Accept and feel your oneness with God. Make a statement below expressing how you experience your oneness with this Presence and Power greater than you are.

(See page 98 for examples of Unification statements.)

3 Maintaining a sense of your unity with a Presence and Power greater than you are, know that Love and Harmony exist in place of your problem with marriage. Contemplate this idea, ridding yourself of all doubt or reservation. Become deeply convinced that the new and positive experience you desire is unfolding for you. Record here the feelings you have as you do this.

Make a positive statement of your changed belief. Write it in the present tense, recognizing and accepting the presence of the Divine qualities of Love and Harmony where your problem appears to be. You are creating a mold for the Universal Law of Mind, so be clear, definite, and specific. Be emphatic! Imagine that what you desire to experience is now established, knowing that it is already taking form in your life through the activity of the Universal Law of Mind. State here what you are now declaring to be true in place of your problem.

(See page 126 for examples of Realization statements.)

4 Recall an occasion in your life when you felt a great outpouring of gratitude — whether for something specific or simply for the joy of being alive. Recapture in your imagination this special time of feeling grateful, and allow the experience to be fresh and vivid for you again. Describe here the feelings you have.

When you have an attitude of thanksgiving, knowing your need is already met, something in this attitude enhances your ability to have faith and to be open and receptive. Right now, completely and wholeheartedly accept that the problem you have in regard to marriage is resolved and feel thankful for this solution. Write a statement here expressing your gratitude.

(See page 154 for examples of Thanksgiving statements.)

5 Have you ever had the experience of feeling completely unburdened, as if a great weight had been lifted from your shoulders? What you felt was a letting go, a release. This is what you need to experience in regard to the problem in your marriage or relationship. Know that the Universal Law of Mind is now creating what you desire. Relax and experience a sense of trust, certain that this resolution is unfolding. Write below what the experience of release feels like.

Sometimes you may tend to doubt or deny the good you want to experience. The act of releasing your affirmative prayer helps prevent that. When you release it, the Universal Law of Mind can freely respond to your new spiritual understanding, revealing Love and Harmony in place of your problem. Right now release all fear and worry, and allow this process to move forward. Let go of the problem and be confident that the good you desire is already unfolding. Write a statement releasing your affirmative prayer to the activity of the Universal Law of Mind.

(See page 182 for examples of Release statements.)

MY AFFIRMATIVE PRAYER

Taken together, the statements you have made at the bottom of the previous five pages comprise a complete affirmative prayer, addressing your particular concern with marriage. This prayer consists of the stages of Recognition, Unification, Realization, Thanksgiving, and Release.

Review each of your five statements now and determine if there are any changes you wish to make in them. As you review them, be sure they evoke deep feeling and conviction in you and are worded concisely for maximum impact. Also be sure they achieve the purpose intended. For example, when you reread your Realization statement, are you able to sense the Love and Harmony of God in your life? After you make any desired changes in your five statements, combine them below into a complete unit.

1 Recognition:

2 Unification:

3 Realization:

4 Thanksgiving:

5 Release:

WHERE DO I GO FROM HERE?

You have now started a process of personal and spiritual growth that will produce new and positive changes for you.

You can do several things to continue the work you started in this section. Stay alert to the statements you make about your situation. At night recall your habitual thought patterns of the day. How much of your thinking was negative and how much was positive? Practice changing the negative statements into positive ones. Say the positive statements over and over until you begin to feel a definite connection with them.

Most important, read your affirmative prayer several times a day. At a minimum, we suggest doing so right before going to bed and upon waking in the morning. Read it out loud if possible. Take time to contemplate it. As you read your prayer and think about it, experience the feelings associated with each of the five stages. Be sure to make reading it meaningful, not simply an automatic exercise. If one of your statements seems to lose impact for you, redo it.

Remain open to change and be willing to follow any inner guidance that comes to you. God works in your life through such inner guidance, which often appears as a new idea or an urge to do something differently. As you allow change to occur, what was originally a problem will be replaced by more desirable circumstances. Remain open-minded and patient, knowing that positive results are certain to take place.

Remember, there is a natural process by which spiritual truth takes form, and the time this process requires varies with different situations. You may have an immediate response to your affirmative prayer or a period of weeks or even months may elapse, but continue with your affirmative prayer, always using the present tense, accepting that what you desire *is now happening*. Keep deepening your level of conviction and adjust the wording of your prayer to reflect your changed state of consciousness. Feel free to create new affirmations and affirmative prayers as your understanding of your unity with God's Love and Harmony expands. Continue with your affirmative prayer until the desired result is obtained.

HOW AM I CHANGING?

Work with the "Old Patterns — New Possibilities" and "Creating My New Life" sections for two to three weeks, then respond to these questions. They will help you assess your progress and guide you if you need assistance. (Since keeping a record of your experiences is useful when you are seeking to improve your life, you may also want to write your continuing insights in a separate notebook.)

■ What changes have you experienced in your situation as a result of working with this section on marriage?

_____

_____

_____

_____

■ Are you satisfied with these results? If you are, what do you think is responsible for your improved circumstances?

_____

_____

_____

_____

■ If you feel you are not making progress, go back over the questions and exercises and your responses to them. Do you need to do something differently? Also look at your affirmative prayer. Does it need to be changed? Be sure to check yourself on negative thought habits. Are you willing to reevaluate your approach and try again?

_____

_____

_____

_____

■ What is the most important thing you have learned about yourself in regard to your marriage or primary relationship?

_____

_____

_____

CHILDRAISING

The solution to most family difficulties lies in having some kind of spiritual faith — a faith in something bigger than we are — bigger than all of us are. But a faith in something that is immediately accessible — a conviction that there is a Living Presence everywhere, a Presence of Good.
                                                    — Ernest Holmes

Most parents at one time or another have to grapple with a wide range of challenges when raising children, from finding good childcare to dealing with the trials of adolescence and confronting the tumultuous emotions when the "child" who seemed only a baby just yesterday leaves home. Some problems involving children can be extremely difficult to deal with: critical illness or injury, serious trouble at school, teenage pregnancy, a run-away child, drug use.

If you are facing any of these circumstances, you may feel there is no help, no solution, no place to turn. But there is help, through affirmative prayer. It offers a definite way for you to bring the Wisdom and Patience of God into any situation you confront.

The spiritual qualities of Wisdom and Patience are present everywhere and are the truth of who you are and who your children are. As you align yourself with the indwelling Presence and Power of God, the activity of the Universal Law of Mind will create the loving and joyous experiences you desire. Understanding and compassion will take the place of discord. You will intuitively know what to do in every situation, and you will have a sense of not being alone — of being guided by an inner Wisdom.

You may not be able to "make" your children be the way you would like them to be, since affirmative prayer is not for the purpose of manipulating other people, but you can create an inner spiritual atmosphere which promotes the well-being of both you and your children.

It may take some time — and it will take some effort — but positive results are bound to occur as you use the following exercises, first to explore your belief patterns and then to develop an affirmative prayer especially designed for your particular problem with raising children.

OLD PATTERNS — NEW POSSIBILITIES

Old Patterns

Your beliefs — which include your thoughts, feelings, and attitudes, both conscious and subconscious — determine what you are now experiencing, for the Universal Law of Mind acts on them to create the circumstances of your life. Use the following exercises to help you become aware of the particular beliefs that underlie your concern about raising children. Take as much time as you need, perhaps a few days, to respond to these questions since they form an important foundation for the work you will be doing to resolve your concern.

■ Look back at "Where Am I Now?" on the subject of childraising (page 19). If you haven't completed that exercise, please do so now. Use the space provided below to answer the following questions: What issues did you respond to with a number 3, 4, or 5? Are these issues related? If so, in what way? Select one of them to work with in this section and note it below.

■ Write down the feelings, especially the fears, you have in regard to this issue. What beliefs can you identify about yourself or about other people that underlie these feelings?

■ What new understanding has come to you as a result of exploring these old belief patterns? On the basis of your new understanding, what would you like to change?

_____

_____

_____

_____

_____

_____

_____

New Possibilities

To break up old patterns of thought and behavior, you need to open yourself to new possibilities. The exercise on the following page, based on contrasting statements, will assist you with this process. Saying the statement in the left column first and then saying the statement in the right column will help you become aware of how you think, and also help you break up habitual non-productive patterns of thinking and expand your consciousness. (Create your own statements if the examples provided do not address your situation.)

When you affirm the statements in either the left or the right column, you are directing the activity of the Universal Law of Mind, which creates your experiences according to the patterns of your thoughts, feelings, and attitudes . . . your beliefs. If these beliefs are consistently negative, your experiences will be negative. If these beliefs are positive, your experiences will be positive. Remember, the Universal Law of Mind does not make choices — *you* make the choices through what you believe. *This means you can consciously choose how to direct the Universal Law of Mind to create the results you want.*

You will be working with these consciousness-expanders as a way of preparing for the next section, "Creating My New Life," in which you use affirmative prayer to deal with your specific concern with raising children. As you read each statement in the right column, see it as a new possibility. Imagine yourself being, acting, and feeling what it expresses. Believe it! Feel the feelings you would have if this statement were actually true right now. In this way you begin the process of changing your thinking.

How do you talk to yourself about your problem? How do you talk to others about it?

If you have been saying:	Now begin to say:
I'm not a very good parent.	I am a capable parent.
I'm afraid my child is on drugs.	My child is not dependent on drugs.
I'm upset over my child's school problems.	I learn how to work with my child.
I don't discipline my children well.	I guide my children wisely.
I don't have enough time with my child.	I spend quality time with my child.
I'm tired of raising my child alone.	I have the help I need to raise my child.
I can't handle my child anymore.	I let love and understanding guide me.
I don't want my children to leave me.	I rejoice in my children's maturity.
How can I provide for clothing, recreation, and college?	Every need is provided for at the right time.
I don't know how to set limits.	My children and I determine limits.
I don't like my visitation rights.	I have satisfactory visitation rights.
My child and I seldom agree.	Harmony exists between me and my child.
I'm unable to cope with my child's illness.	I have the strength and support I need.
I can't get a divorce because of the children.	I alone am responsible for a decision to divorce.
My spouse and I fight about childraising.	My spouse and I discuss our differences.
The baby puts stress on our marriage.	Our marriage is strong and loving.
Raising children is a burden.	Children are a joy and a privilege.
I don't have any time for myself.	I have time for myself each day.
I'm afraid I neglect my children.	I give loving attention to my children.
I don't know where my child is.	My child is safe and well.
Other_____ (use additional paper if necessary)	_____

Now turn to the next section, "Creating My New Life," to learn to use affirmative prayer to deal with your specific issue related to raising your children.

DAILY AFFIRMATION:

I have the wisdom and patience I need to successfully raise my children.

CREATING MY NEW LIFE

In the previous section you started to see that the Universal Law of Mind acts on your beliefs to create your experiences. You began to identify and break free from negative patterns of belief and you are now aware of new possibilities. *Incorporating any additional understanding you gained in that section, write here what you want your new experience to be.*

_____

_____

_____

_____

This portion of the workbook will help you learn how to create an affirmative prayer to resolve the problem you have in regard to your children. In affirmative prayer, you align your thinking with the Divine qualities of Wisdom and Patience already inherent within you. When you do this, your experience changes. This change occurs as the Universal Law of Mind acts on your new beliefs. (Remember, when we say "beliefs" we mean thoughts, feelings, and attitudes, both conscious and subconscious.)

Realizing through affirmative prayer that Wisdom and Patience are the truth about God and that you are unified with God, you come to know that wisdom and patience are also the truth about you in regard to raising your children. As a result, problems are resolved.

Each of the following exercises has two parts. The first part consists of an activity which helps prepare you to write your affirmative prayer. This activity is designed to assist you in developing an inner atmosphere of strong feeling and conviction, one that will make your statements effective. The second part involves actually writing the five stages of your affirmative prayer. Through this process, as you align your thinking with what is true about God, a solution to your childraising problem unfolds.

Each of the five stages of affirmative prayer — Recognition, Unification, Realization, Thanksgiving, and Release — is explained fully on the following pages: page 70 (Recognition), page 98 (Unification), page 126 (Realization), page 154 (Thanksgiving), and page 182 (Release). Examples are also provided. Be sure to refer to these examples for guidance and suggestions.

1 There is one Presence and one Power, which exists everywhere in the world. It is evident in the wondrous cycle of creation as new life continually emerges. Look closely at a flower and sense the Presence and Power of God expressing in it. Especially sense the Divine Wisdom that designed it and the Divine Patience that lovingly nurtures and sustains it. Recognizing the presence of Wisdom and Patience everywhere, become aware of the activity of God's Power in the world around you. Write in the space below what you think and feel about this Presence and Power.

_____

_____

_____

_____

_____

_____

_____

_____

_____

There is a Presence and Power greater than you are — God — which is the Source and the Creator of everything around you. Recognize that there is one God, one Life, one Mind and that it is ever present, ever active, and constantly creative. Now state what you have recognized, letting your statement be as sincere and meaningful as you can.

_____

_____

_____

_____

_____

(See page 70 for examples of Recognition statements.)

2 As you observe the Presence and Power of God everywhere around you, begin to experience your deep connection with God. Know you are part of God. Know there is one Life, that Life is God, and that Life is what you are. Know there is one Universal Law of Mind which always responds to your beliefs. Feel your oneness with the Divine qualities of Wisdom and Patience, taking time to sense the presence of these qualities within you. When have you felt guided by an intuitive wisdom or calmed by an understanding patience? Remember these occasions and reflect on them. Become still and know that as a spiritual being you are not separate from God-Life, nor are you separate from the Power that gives form to Divine qualities. Write in the space below what this experience of unification feels like.

Observing the Presence and the Power of God everywhere around you, become aware that you are part of a great Unity. Accept and feel your oneness with God. Make a statement below expressing how you experience your oneness with this Presence and Power greater than you are.

(See page 98 for examples of Unification statements.)

3 Maintaining a sense of your unity with a Presence and Power greater than you are, know that Wisdom and Patience exist in place of your problem with raising children. Contemplate this idea, ridding yourself of all doubt or reservation. Become deeply convinced that the new and positive experience you desire is unfolding for you. Record here the feelings you have as you do this.

_____

_____

_____

_____

_____

_____

_____

_____

_____

_____

Make a positive statement of your changed belief. Write it in the present tense, recognizing and accepting the presence of the Divine qualities of Wisdom and Patience where your problem appears to be. You are creating a mold for the Universal Law of Mind, so be clear, definite, and specific. Be emphatic! Imagine that what you desire to experience is now established, knowing that it is already taking form in your life through the activity of the Universal Law of Mind. State here what you are now declaring to be true in place of your problem with raising children.

_____

_____

_____

_____

(See page 126 for examples of Realization statements.)

4 Recall an occasion in your life when you felt a great outpouring of gratitude — whether for something specific or simply for the joy of being alive. Recapture in your imagination this special time of feeling grateful, and allow the experience to be fresh and vivid for you again. Describe here the feelings you have.

When you have an attitude of thanksgiving, knowing your need is already met, something in this attitude enhances your ability to have faith and to be open and receptive. Right now, completely and wholeheartedly accept that your problem with raising children is resolved and feel thankful for this solution. Write a statement here expressing your gratitude.

(See page 154 for examples of Thanksgiving statements.)

5 Have you ever had the experience of feeling completely unburdened, as if a great weight had been lifted from your shoulders? What you felt was a letting go, a release. This is what you need to experience in regard to the problem you have with raising your children. Know that the Universal Law of Mind is now creating what you desire. Relax and experience a sense of trust, certain that this resolution is unfolding. Write below what the experience of release feels like.

_____

_____

_____

_____

_____

_____

_____

_____

_____

_____

Sometimes you may tend to doubt or deny the good you want to experience. The act of releasing your affirmative prayer helps prevent that. When you release it, the Universal Law of Mind can freely respond to your new spiritual understanding, revealing Wisdom and Patience in place of your concern. Right now release all fear and worry, and allow this process to move forward. Let go of the problem and be confident that the good you desire is already unfolding. Write a statement releasing your affirmative prayer to the activity of the Universal Law of Mind.

_____

_____

_____

_____

(See page 182 for examples of Release statements.)

MY AFFIRMATIVE PRAYER

Taken together, the statements you have made at the bottom of the previous five pages comprise a complete affirmative prayer, addressing the particular concern about raising children you have chosen to deal with. This prayer consists of the stages of Recognition, Unification, Realization, Thanksgiving, and Release.

Review each of your five statements now and determine if there are any changes you wish to make in them. As you review them, be sure they evoke deep feeling and conviction in you and are worded concisely for maximum impact. Also be sure they achieve the purpose intended. For example, when you reread your Realization statement, are you able to sense the Wisdom and Patience of God in your life? After you make any desired changes in your five statements, combine them below into a complete unit.

1 Recognition: _____

_____

2 Unification: _____

_____

_____

3 Realization: _____

_____

_____

4 Thanksgiving: _____

_____

_____

5 Release: _____

_____

_____

WHERE DO I GO FROM HERE?

You have now started a process of personal and spiritual growth that will produce the new and positive changes you desire.

You can do several things to continue the work you started in this section. Stay alert to the statements you make about your situation. At night recall your habitual thought patterns of the day. How much of your thinking was negative and how much was positive? Practice changing the negative statements into positive ones. Say the positive statements over and over until you begin to feel a definite connection with them.

Most important, read your affirmative prayer several times a day. At a minimum, we suggest doing so right before going to bed and upon waking in the morning. Read it out loud if possible. Take time to contemplate it. As you read your prayer and think about it, experience the feelings associated with each of the five stages. Be sure to make reading it meaningful, not simply an automatic exercise. If one of your statements seems to lose impact for you, redo it.

Remain open to change and be willing to follow any inner guidance that comes to you. God works in your life through such inner guidance, which often appears as a new idea or an urge to do something differently. As you allow change to occur, what was originally a problem will be replaced by more desirable circumstances. Remain open-minded and patient, knowing that positive results are certain to take place.

Remember, there is a natural process by which spiritual truth takes form, and the time this process requires varies with different situations. You may have an immediate response to your affirmative prayer or a period of weeks or even months may elapse, but continue with your affirmative prayer, always using the present tense, accepting that what you desire *is now happening*. Keep deepening your level of conviction and adjust the wording of your prayer to reflect your changed state of consciousness. Feel free to create new affirmations and affirmative prayers as your understanding of your unity with God's Wisdom and Patience expands. Continue with your affirmative prayer until the desired result is obtained.

HOW AM I CHANGING?

Work with the "Old Patterns — New Possibilities" and "Creating My New Life" sections for two to three weeks, then respond to these questions. They will help you assess your progress and guide you if you need assistance. (Since keeping a record of your experiences is useful when you are seeking to improve your life, you may also want to write your continuing insights in a separate notebook.)

■ What changes have you experienced in your situation as a result of working with this section on childraising?

_____

_____

_____

_____

■ Are you satisfied with these results? If you are, what do you think is responsible for your improved circumstances?

_____

_____

_____

_____

■ If you feel you are not making progress, go back over the questions and exercises and your responses to them. Do you need to do something differently? Also look at your affirmative prayer. Does it need to be changed? Be sure to check yourself on negative thought habits. Are you willing to reevaluate your approach and try again?

_____

_____

_____

■ What is the most important thing you have learned about yourself in regard to raising children?

_____

_____

_____

UNIFICATION

Unification is the second stage of affirmative prayer. In this stage, having recognized God as the ultimate Presence and Power in and through everything, you accept that you and God are one. The life within you is God. You are never separate from the loving Presence of God. God is the creative Power of your life.

Purpose of the Unification stage of an affirmative prayer: To know and understand that since God is everything you also must be part of God; to become aware that you are a unique, individual expression of God and to know that all good is already yours.

Suggestions for creating an effective statement of unification: In a statement of unification you express your oneness with the Divine Presence and Power. Consciously sense and feel the Divine Presence not only within you but also as what you are. The reasoning process to use is: God is everything; I am part of everything; therefore, I am part of God. Eliminate any sense of separation between you and God, and as you let go of feelings of separation, fill yourself with thoughts of oneness. What does this oneness, this unity, mean to you? In contemplating the idea that the Divine Presence is at the center of your being, identify yourself with qualities of God — Love, Peace, Wisdom, Wholeness, Harmony. Know that everything you think about and do is supported by this Divine Presence.

When you have felt your oneness with God as fully as you can, begin to make your statement of unification, letting it come forth with the deepest sense of conviction you have. You are stating the truth about you so let your statement affirm this truth as strongly as possible. Record your statement on the appropriate page of this workbook.

Examples of Unification Statements:

☐ I know I am one with God. God is within me and God's action guides and directs me at all times. I accept this unity completely and let a sense of oneness with the Divine Presence and Power fill my being.

☐ Knowing the Divine Presence and Power within me, as me, is the truth of my nature, I let go of any sense of separation and joyfully embrace my newly recognized unity with all that God is.

☐ My life is Divinely created and sustained. I am one with the infinite Presence and Power and I now totally open myself to the inflow of this Divine Life.

PARENTS

I believe we are all one family in God, and that God is working in each of us in such a way that there will be produced a better family, a better nation, a better world.
        — Ernest Holmes

As an adult, you begin to see your parents more objectively than you did when you were a small child. While they once may have seemed either infallible or deficient to you, now you are able to view them more realistically, as people with their own hopes and fears, strengths and weaknesses, hurts and joys . . . people who were doing the best they could to be good parents to you when you were younger.

However, despite your new understanding, you may find that your life is still affected by your childhood relationship with your parents. For example, a tendency to let yourself be dependent on others may persist, you may be intimidated by people in authority, or you may be plagued by guilt feelings over some past behavior disapproved of by your parents.

The problem you now face may be something that has arisen recently rather than having its origin in the past. Perhaps you have become responsible for the care of an aging parent and are finding this to be a burden, or your parents have divorced and you feel hurt and betrayed.

There is a solution. As you use affirmative prayer, recognizing your unity with the Harmony and Balance of God, you begin to experience greater harmony and balance in the situation regarding your parents. By knowing you are one with the Presence and Power of God and by changing your belief patterns from negative to positive, you redirect the activity of the Universal Law of Mind.

Use the exercises on the following pages to help you uncover negative patterns of thinking and feeling, and to guide you in creating an affirmative prayer for a more harmonious relationship with your parents.

OLD PATTERNS — NEW POSSIBILITIES

Old Patterns

Your beliefs — which include your thoughts, feelings, and attitudes, both conscious and subconscious — determine what you are now experiencing, for the Universal Law of Mind acts on them to create the circumstances of your life. Use the following exercises to help you become aware of the particular beliefs that underlie your concern about your relationship with your parents. Take as much time as you need, perhaps a few days, to respond to these questions since they form an important foundation for the work you will be doing to resolve this concern.

■ Look back at "Where Am I Now?" on the subject of parents (page 20). If you haven't completed that exercise, please do so now. Use the space provided below to answer the following questions: What issues did you respond to with a number 3, 4, or 5? Are these issues related? If so, in what way? Select one of them to work with in this section and note it below.

■ Write down the feelings, especially the fears, you have in regard to this issue. What beliefs can you identify about yourself or about other people that underlie these feelings?

■ What new understanding has come to you as a result of exploring these old belief patterns? On the basis of your new understanding, what would you like to change?

_____

_____

_____

_____

_____

_____

_____

_____

New Possibilities

To break up old patterns of thought and behavior, you need to open yourself to new possibilities. The exercise on the following page, based on contrasting statements, will assist you with this process. Saying the statement in the left column first and then saying the statement in the right column will help you become aware of how you think, and also help you break up habitual non-productive patterns of thinking and expand your consciousness. (Create your own statements if the examples provided do not address your situation.)

When you affirm the statements in either the left or the right column, you are directing the activity of the Universal Law of Mind, which creates your experiences according to the patterns of your thoughts, feelings, and attitudes . . . your beliefs. If these beliefs are consistently negative, your experiences will be negative. If these beliefs are positive, your experiences will be positive. Remember, the Universal Law of Mind does not make choices — *you* make the choices through what you believe. *This means you can consciously choose how to direct the Universal Law of Mind to create the results you want.*

You will be working with these consciousness-expanders as a way of preparing for the next section, "Creating My New Life," in which you use affirmative prayer to deal with your specific concern with respect to your parents. As you read each statement in the right column, see it as a new possibility. Imagine yourself being, acting, and feeling what it expresses. Believe it! Feel the feelings you would have if this statement were actually true right now. In this way you begin the process of changing your thinking.

How do you talk to yourself about your concern? How do you talk to others about it?

If you have been saying:

Now begin to say:

If you have been saying:	Now begin to say:
My parents treat me like a child.	I lovingly make my own decisions.
My mother still wants to control me.	I am independent of my mother.
My parents are a financial burden to me.	I lovingly share with my parents.
I'm angry over my parents' divorce.	I accept my parents' divorce.
My parents never understand me.	I understand my parents better.
I'm worn out by my parent's illness.	I ask for help when necessary.
I can't forgive my parent for drinking.	I understand my parent and love him/her.
My parents and I always argue.	We now talk without arguing.
I worry about my parents' aging.	I accept growing older as part of life.
My parents won't give me money anymore.	I enjoy taking care of myself.
I wish I'd been nicer to my parents while they were still living.	Today I understand and forgive myself for any past actions.
My parents want to be dependent on me.	I am independent yet helpful to them.
My parents ask too many questions.	My parents' interest is a form of love.
I don't like my parent's new spouse.	I choose to like my parent's spouse.
My parents did some bad things to me.	I live in this moment, forgiving the past.
I'll never be able to satisfy my parents.	The only person I must satisfy is myself.
My parents live their lives through me.	I accept my freedom and autonomy.
I'll never resolve my conflicts with my parents.	I accept the peaceful resolution of conflicts with my parents.
My parent's living with us keeps me tied down.	I ask family and friends for help when I need it.
I don't want to have to put my parent in a nursing home.	I accept the most appropriate care for my parent.

Other_____   _____
(use additional paper if necessary)

Now turn to the next section, "Creating My New Life," to learn to use affirmative prayer to deal with your specific issue relating to parents.

DAILY AFFIRMATION:

I experience harmony and balance in my relationship with my parents.

CREATING MY NEW LIFE

In the previous section you started to see that the Universal Law of Mind acts on your beliefs to create your experiences. You began to identify and break free from negative patterns of belief and you are now aware of new possibilities. *Incorporating any additional understanding you gained in that section, write here what you want your new experience to be.*

_____

_____

_____

_____

This portion of the workbook will help you learn how to create an affirmative prayer to resolve the concern you have regarding your parents. In affirmative prayer, you align your thinking with the Divine qualities of Harmony and Balance already inherent within you. When you do this, your experience changes. This change occurs as the Universal Law of Mind acts on your new beliefs. (Remember, when we say "beliefs" we mean thoughts, feelings, and attitudes, both conscious and subconscious.)

Realizing through affirmative prayer that Harmony and Balance are the truth about God and that you are unified with God, you come to know that harmony and balance are also the truth about you and your relationship with your parents. As a result, problems are resolved.

Each of the following exercises has two parts. The first part consists of an activity which helps prepare you to write your affirmative prayer. This activity is designed to assist you in developing an inner atmosphere of strong feeling and conviction, one that will make your statements effective. The second part involves actually writing the five stages of your affirmative prayer. Through this process, as you align your thinking with what is true about God, a solution to your concern regarding your parents unfolds.

Each of the five stages of affirmative prayer — Recognition, Unification, Realization, Thanksgiving, and Release — is explained fully on the following pages: page 70 (Recognition), page 98 (Unification), page 126 (Realization), page 154 (Thanksgiving), and page 182 (Release). Examples are also provided. Be sure to refer to these examples for guidance and suggestions.

1 A perfect Presence and Power exists in the universe, the infinite Life of God. This life expresses in many ways, including as Harmony and Balance. Observe these Divine qualities in evidence in the world around you. Notice, for example, how many different forms of life exist together in harmonious relationship. Recognizing the Divine qualities of Harmony and Balance everywhere, become aware of the creative activity of God's Power in the world around you. Write in the space below what you think and feel about this Presence and Power.

There is a Presence and Power greater than you are — God — which is the Source and the Creator of everything around you. Recognize that there is one God, one Life, one Mind and that it is ever present, ever active, and constantly creative. Now state what you have recognized, letting your statement be as sincere and meaningful as you can.

(See page 70 for examples of Recognition statements.)

2 As you observe the Presence and Power of God everywhere around you, begin now to experience your deep connection with God. Know you are part of God. Know there is one Life, that Life is God, and that Life is what you are. Know there is one Universal Law of Mind which always responds to your beliefs. Feel your oneness with the Divine qualities of Harmony and Balance, taking time to sense the presence of these qualities within you. When have you experienced feelings of harmony and balance in your life? Remember these occasions and reflect on them. Become still and know that as a spiritual being you are not separate from God-Life, nor are you separate from the Power that gives form to Divine qualities. Write in the space below what this experience of unification feels like.

Observing the Presence and the Power of God everywhere around you, become aware that you are part of a great Unity. Accept and feel your oneness with God. Make a statement below expressing how you experience your oneness with this Presence and Power greater than you are.

(See page 98 for examples of Unification statements.)

3 Maintaining a sense of your unity with a Presence and Power greater than you are, know that Balance and Harmony exist in place of the problem you have with your parents. Contemplate this idea, ridding yourself of all doubt or reservation. Become deeply convinced that the new and positive experience you desire is unfolding for you. Record here the feelings you have as you do this.

_____

_____

_____

_____

_____

_____

_____

_____

_____

_____

Make a positive statement of your changed belief. Write it in the present tense, recognizing and accepting the presence of the Divine qualities of Balance and Harmony where your problem appears to be. You are creating a mold for the Universal Law of Mind, so be clear, definite, and specific. Be emphatic! Imagine that what you desire to experience is now established, knowing that it is already taking form in your life through the activity of the Universal Law of Mind. State here what you are now declaring to be true in place of your problem.

_____

_____

_____

_____

_____

(See page 126 for examples of Realization statements.)

4 Recall an occasion in your life when you felt a great outpouring of gratitude — whether for something specific or simply for the joy of being alive. Recapture in your imagination this special time of feeling grateful, and allow the experience to be fresh and vivid for you again. Describe here the feelings you have.

_____

_____

_____

_____

_____

_____

_____

_____

_____

_____

_____

_____

When you have an attitude of thanksgiving, knowing your need is already met, something in this attitude enhances your ability to have faith and to be open and receptive. Right now, completely and wholeheartedly accept that your concern involving your parents is resolved and feel thankful for this solution. Write a statement here expressing your gratitude.

_____

_____

_____

_____

_____

(See page 154 for examples of Thanksgiving statements.)

5 Have you ever had the experience of feeling completely unburdened, as if a great weight had been lifted from your shoulders? What you felt was a letting go, a release. This is what you need to experience in regard to your concern with your parents. Know that the Universal Law of Mind is now creating what you desire. Relax and experience a sense of trust, certain that this resolution is unfolding. Write below what the experience of release feels like.

Sometimes you may tend to doubt or deny the good you want to experience. The act of releasing your affirmative prayer helps prevent that. When you release it, the Universal Law of Mind can freely respond to your new spiritual understanding, revealing Harmony and Balance in place of the problem you have regarding your parents. Right now release all fear and worry, and allow this process to move forward. Let go of the problem and be confident that the good you desire is already unfolding. Write a statement releasing your affirmative prayer to the activity of the Universal Law of Mind.

(See page 182 for examples of Release statements.)

MY AFFIRMATIVE PRAYER

Taken together, the statements you have made at the bottom of the previous five pages comprise a complete affirmative prayer, addressing the particular concern with respect to your parents you have chosen to deal with. This prayer consists of the stages of Recognition, Unification, Realization, Thanksgiving, and Release.

Review each of your five statements now and determine if there are any changes you wish to make in them. As you review them, be sure they evoke deep feeling and conviction in you and are worded concisely for maximum impact. Also be sure they achieve the purpose intended. For example, when you reread your Realization statement, are you able to sense the Harmony and Balance of God in your life? After you make any desired changes in your five statements, combine them below into a complete unit.

1 Recognition:

2 Unification:

3 Realization:

4 Thanksgiving:

5 Release:

WHERE DO I GO FROM HERE?

You have now started a process of personal and spiritual growth that will produce new and positive changes for you.

You can do several things to continue the work you started in this section. Stay alert to the statements you make about your situation. At night recall your habitual thought patterns of the day. How much of your thinking was negative and how much was positive? Practice changing the negative statements into positive ones. Say the positive statements over and over until you begin to feel a definite connection with them.

Most important, read your affirmative prayer several times a day. At a minimum, we suggest doing so right before going to bed and upon waking in the morning. Read it out loud if possible. Take time to contemplate it. As you read your prayer and think about it, experience the feelings associated with each of the five stages. Be sure to make reading it meaningful, not simply an automatic exercise. If one of your statements seems to lose impact for you, redo it.

Remain open to change and be willing to follow any inner guidance that comes to you. God works in your life through such inner guidance, which often appears as a new idea or an urge to do something differently. As you allow change to occur, what was originally a problem will be replaced by more desirable circumstances. Remain open-minded and patient, knowing that positive results are certain to take place.

Remember, there is a natural process by which spiritual truth takes form, and the time this process requires varies with different situations. You may have an immediate response to your affirmative prayer or a period of weeks or even months may elapse, but continue your affirmative prayer, always using the present tense, accepting that what you desire *is happening now*. Keep deepening your level of conviction and adjust the wording of your prayer to reflect your changed state of consciousness. Feel free to create new affirmations and affirmative prayers as your understanding of your unity with God's Harmony and Balance expands. Continue with your affirmative prayer until the desired result is obtained.

HOW AM I CHANGING?

Work with the "Old Patterns — New Possibilities" and "Creating My New Life" sections for two to three weeks, then respond to these questions. They will help you assess your progress and guide you if you need assistance. (Since keeping a record of your experiences is useful when you are seeking to improve your life, you may also want to write your continuing insights in a separate notebook.)

■ What changes have you experienced in your situation as a result of working with this section on parents?

_____

_____

_____

■ Are you satisfied with these results? If you are, what do you think is responsible for your improved circumstances?

_____

_____

_____

■ If you feel you are not making progress, go back over the questions and exercises and your responses to them. Do you need to do something differently? Also look at your affirmative prayer. Does it need to be changed? Be sure to check yourself on negative thought habits. Are you willing to reevaluate your approach and try again?

_____

_____

_____

■ What is the most important thing you have learned about yourself in regard to your relationship with your parents?

_____

_____

_____

FRIENDSHIP

There is some part of you which reaches into the nature of others, thus irresistibly drawing them to you and drawing you to them, binding all together in one complete unity. Right now you are one with all persons, all places, all events.
— Ernest Holmes

Life is meant to be shared with others, and one way such sharing takes place is through friendship. Not only does friendship provide opportunities to participate deeply in the life of another person, but it also offers an avenue for learning more about your own humanness and for expressing more fully the qualities of God inherent within you.

Friendship begins within you, with your thoughts, feelings, and attitudes — your beliefs. If you are not happy with your current relationships, become willing to explore these beliefs. To bring about more rewarding experiences, you need to adopt beliefs that foster feelings of love, kindness, understanding, and sincerity and at the same time you need to eliminate all beliefs that result in feelings of jealousy, competition, envy, or resentment. By thus directing your thinking in a positive, God-centered way, you cause the Universal Law of Mind to create the loving and fulfilling friendships you desire.

Remember that while the bond between friends may become strained at times through misunderstandings or unrealistic expectations, the friendship can survive and even become stronger when both persons are willing to search honestly for the causes and to work toward restoring and revitalizing the relationship.

A wonderful way to resolve a conflict with a friend or to bring new friendship into your life is through affirmative prayer. As you use this approach, you build a deep conviction of your unity with the Presence and Power of God, and you allow the Divine qualities of Warmth and Acceptance to express more freely through you. When you do so, sensing your unity with all people, you discover that any problem you have with friendship can be resolved.

Keep in mind when you work with the following exercises that as you enrich your life through friendships you will also be enriching the lives of others.

OLD PATTERNS — NEW POSSIBILITIES

Old Patterns

Your beliefs — which include your thoughts, feelings, and attitudes, both conscious and subconscious — determine what you are now experiencing, for the Universal Law of Mind acts on them to create the circumstances of your life. Use the following exercises to help you become aware of the particular beliefs that underlie the problem you are having with friendship. Take as much time as you need, perhaps a few days, to respond to these questions since they form an important foundation for the work you will be doing to resolve your problem.

■ Look back at "Where Am I Now?" on the subject of friendship (page 21). If you haven't completed that exercise, please do so now. Use the space provided below to answer the following questions: What issues did you respond to with a number 3, 4, or 5? Are these issues related? If so, in what way? Select one of them to work with in this section and note it below.

■ Write down the feelings, especially the fears, you have in regard to this issue. What beliefs can you identify about yourself or about other people that underlie these feelings?

■ What new understanding has come to you as a result of exploring these old belief patterns? On the basis of your new understanding, what would you like to change?

_____

_____

_____

_____

_____

_____

_____

_____

New Possibilities

To break up old patterns of thought and behavior, you need to open yourself to new possibilities. The exercise on the following page, based on contrasting statements, will assist you with this process. Saying the statement in the left column first and then saying the statement in the right column will help you become aware of how you think, and also help you break up habitual non-productive patterns of thinking and expand your consciousness. (Create your own statements if the examples provided do not address your situation.)

When you affirm the statements in either the left or the right column, you are directing the activity of the Universal Law of Mind, which creates your experiences according to the patterns of your thoughts, feelings, and attitudes . . . your beliefs. If these beliefs are consistently negative, your experiences will be negative. If these beliefs are positive, your experiences will be positive. Remember, the Universal Law of Mind does not make choices — *you* make the choices through what you believe. *This means you can consciously choose how to direct the Universal Law of Mind to create the results you want.*

You will be working with these consciousness-expanders as a way of preparing for the next section, "Creating My New Life," in which you use affirmative prayer to deal with your specific concern with friendship. As you read each statement in the right column, see it as a new possibility. Imagine yourself being, acting, and feeling what it expresses. Believe it! Feel the feelings you would have if this statement were actually true right now. In this way you begin the process of changing your thinking.

How do you talk to yourself about your problem? How do you talk to others about it?

If you have been saying:

I have trouble keeping friends.

I don't know how to make new friends.

I let friends take advantage of me.

I'm afraid of close friendships.

I feel left out by friends.

I envy my friend's clothes and new car.

I am upset with my competitive friend.

I'm afraid my friends will reject me.

I can't express anger to friends.

I'm not a very good friend.

I'm not as attractive as my friends.

My friends only like me for my money.

I don't need friends.

Friends often let me down.

I can't break away from bad friendships.

My friend won't open up but expects me to.

I'm afraid my friend will leave me.

I don't like my friend anymore.

My friend is demanding and manipulative.

I don't want to share my friend with others.

Other_____
(use additional paper if necessary)

Now begin to say:

I keep friends by being a good friend.

I reach out to people in friendship.

I set appropriate limits with friends.

I open myself to warmth and love.

I am a valued friend.

I am happy for my friend's success.

I discuss my feelings with my friend.

I am loved and accepted by my friends.

I honestly express my feelings.

I am a warm, companionable friend.

I am attractive in my special way.

I am liked for myself.

I have a true friend.

I release my expectations of others.

I make a clean break from bad friendships.

I share my feelings unconditionally.

I lovingly support my friend's choice.

I accept the changes in me.

I make my own choices.

I open my life to other friends and activities.

_____

Now turn to the next section, "Creating My New Life," to learn to use affirmative prayer to deal with your specific issue relating to friendship.

DAILY AFFIRMATION:

I experience warmth and acceptance in all of my friendships.

CREATING MY NEW LIFE

In the previous section you started to see that the Universal Law of Mind acts on your beliefs to create your experiences. You began to identify and break free from negative patterns of belief and you are now aware of new possibilities. *Incorporating any additional understanding you gained in that section, write here what you want your new experience to be.*

_____

_____

_____

_____

This portion of the workbook will help you learn how to create an affirmative prayer to resolve your concern with friendship. In affirmative prayer, you align your thinking with the Divine qualities of Warmth and Acceptance already inherent within you. When you do this, your experience changes. This change occurs as the Universal Law of Mind acts on your new beliefs. (Remember, when we say ''beliefs'' we mean thoughts, feelings, and attitudes, both conscious and subconscious.)

Realizing through affirmative prayer that Warmth and Acceptance are the truth about God and that you are unified with God, you come to know that warmth and acceptance are also the truth about you in regard to friendship. As a result, problems are resolved.

Each of the following exercises has two parts. The first part consists of an activity which helps prepare you to write your affirmative prayer. This activity is designed to assist you in developing an inner atmosphere of strong feeling and conviction, one that will make your statements effective. The second part involves actually writing the five stages of your affirmative prayer. Through this process, as you align your thinking with what is true about God, a solution to your concern unfolds.

Each of the five stages of affirmative prayer — Recognition, Unification, Realization, Thanksgiving, and Release — is explained fully on the following pages: page 70 (Recognition), page 98 (Unification), page 126 (Realization), page 154 (Thanksgiving), and page 182 (Release). Examples are also provided. Be sure to refer to these examples for guidance and suggestions.

1 The loving Presence and Power of God exists everywhere in the universe. This perfect Life is evident in affectionate companionship, joyous sharing, and kind support. It is also evident in a principle of affinity that operates in the world, bringing like things together and maintaining the essential unity of all of life. Observe examples of this principle operating: children at play, rivulets of water merging after a rain, newborn kittens snuggling close. As you observe the Acceptance and Warmth of God being revealed in these and other ways, recognize the activity of God's Power in the world around you. Write in the space below what you think and feel about this Presence and Power.

There is a Presence and Power greater than you are — God — which is the Source and the Creator of everything around you. Recognize that there is one God, one Life, one Mind and that it is ever present, ever active, and constantly creative. Now state what you have recognized, letting your statement be as sincere and meaningful as you can.

(See page 70 for examples of Recognition statements.)

2 As you observe the Presence and Power of God everywhere around you, begin to experience your deep connection with God. Know you are part of God. Know there is one Life, that Life is God, and that Life is what you are. Know there is one Universal Law of Mind which always responds to your beliefs. Feel your oneness with the Divine qualities of Warmth and Acceptance, taking time to sense the presence of these qualities within you. When have you been filled with a sense of loving warmth and open acceptance toward someone? Remember these occasions and reflect on them. Become still and know that as a spiritual being you are not separate from God-Life, nor are you separate from the Power that gives form to Divine qualities. Write in the space below what this experience of unification feels like.

_____

_____

_____

_____

_____

_____

_____

_____

_____

_____

Observing the Presence and the Power of God everywhere around you, become aware that you are part of a great Unity. Accept and feel your oneness with God. Make a statement below expressing how you experience your oneness with this Presence and Power greater than you are.

_____

_____

_____

_____

_____

_____

(See page 98 for examples of Unification statements.)

3 Maintaining a sense of your unity with a Presence and Power greater than you are, know that Warmth and Acceptance exist in place of the problem you are having with friendship. Contemplate this idea, ridding yourself of all doubt or reservation. Become deeply convinced that the new and positive experience you desire is unfolding for you. Record here the feelings you have as you do this.

_____

_____

_____

_____

_____

_____

_____

_____

_____

Make a positive statement of your changed belief. Write it in the present tense, recognizing and accepting the presence of the Divine qualities of Warmth and Acceptance where your problem appears to be. You are creating a mold for the Universal Law of Mind, so be clear, definite, and specific. Be emphatic! Imagine that what you desire to experience is now established, knowing that it is already taking form in your life through the activity of the Universal Law of Mind. State here what you are now declaring to be true in place of your problem.

_____

_____

_____

_____

_____

(See page 126 for examples of Realization statements.)

4 Recall an occasion in your life when you felt a great outpouring of gratitude — whether for something specific or simply for the joy of being alive. Recapture in your imagination this special time of feeling grateful, and allow the experience to be fresh and vivid for you again. Describe here the feelings you have.

When you have an attitude of thanksgiving, knowing your need is already met, something in this attitude enhances your ability to have faith and to be open and receptive. Right now, completely and wholeheartedly accept that your problem with friendship is resolved and feel thankful for this solution. Write a statement here expressing your gratitude.

(See page 154 for examples of Thanksgiving statements.)

5 Have you ever had the experience of feeling completely unburdened, as if a great weight had been lifted from your shoulders? What you felt was a letting go, a release. This is what you need to experience in regard to your problem with friendship. Know that the Universal Law of Mind is now creating what you desire. Relax and experience a sense of trust, certain that this resolution is unfolding. Write below what the experience of release feels like.

_____

_____

_____

_____

_____

_____

_____

_____

_____

_____

_____

Sometimes you may tend to doubt or deny the good you want to experience. The act of releasing your affirmative prayer helps prevent that. When you release it, the Universal Law of Mind can freely respond to your new spiritual understanding, revealing Warmth and Acceptance in place of your concern. Right now release all fear and worry, and allow this process to move forward. Let go of the problem and be confident that the good you desire is already unfolding. Write a statement releasing your affirmative prayer to the activity of the Universal Law of Mind.

_____

_____

_____

_____

(See page 182 for examples of Release statements.)

MY AFFIRMATIVE PRAYER

Taken together, the statements you have made at the bottom of the previous five pages comprise a complete affirmative prayer, addressing the particular concern you have chosen to deal with. This prayer consists of the stages of Recognition, Unification, Realization, Thanksgiving, and Release.

Review each of your five statements now and determine if there are any changes you wish to make in them. As you review them, be sure they evoke deep feeling and conviction in you and are worded concisely for maximum impact. Also be sure they achieve the purpose intended. For example, when you reread your Realization statement, are you able to sense the Acceptance and Warmth of God in your life? After you make any desired changes in your five statements, combine them below into a complete unit.

1 Recognition:

2 Unification:

3 Realization:

4 Thanksgiving:

5 Release:

WHERE DO I GO FROM HERE?

You have now started a process of personal and spiritual growth that will produce new and positive changes for you.

You can do several things to continue the work you started in this section. Stay alert to the statements you make about your situation. At night recall your habitual thought patterns of the day. How much of your thinking was negative and how much was positive? Practice changing the negative statements into positive ones. Say the positive statements over and over until you begin to feel a definite connection with them.

Most important, read your affirmative prayer several times a day. At a minimum, we suggest doing so right before going to bed and upon waking in the morning. Read it out loud if possible. Take time to contemplate it. As you read your prayer and think about it, experience the feelings associated with each of the five stages. Be sure to make reading it meaningful, not simply an automatic exercise. If one of your statements seems to lose impact for you, redo it.

Remain open to change and be willing to follow any inner guidance that comes to you. God works in your life through such inner guidance, which often appears as a new idea or an urge to do something differently. As you allow change to occur, what was originally a problem will be replaced by more desirable circumstances. Remain open-minded and patient, knowing that positive results are certain to take place.

Remember, there is a natural process by which spiritual truth takes form, and the time this process requires varies with different situations. You may have an immediate response to your affirmative prayer or a period of weeks or even months may elapse, but continue with your affirmative prayer, always using the present tense, accepting that what you desire *is now happening*. Keep deepening your level of conviction and adjust the wording of your prayer to reflect your changed state of consciousness. Feel free to create new affirmations and affirmative prayers as your understanding of your unity with God's Warmth and Acceptance expands. Continue with your affirmative prayer until the desired result is obtained.

HOW AM I CHANGING?

Work with the "Old Patterns — New Possibilities" and "Creating My New Life" sections for two to three weeks, then respond to these questions. They will help you assess your progress and guide you if you need assistance. (Since keeping a record of your experiences is useful when you are seeking to improve your life, you may also want to write your continuing insights in a separate notebook.)

■ What changes have you experienced in your situation as a result of working with this section on friendship?

_____

_____

_____

■ Are you satisfied with these results? If you are, what do you think is responsible for your improved circumstances?

_____

_____

_____

■ If you feel you are not making progress, go back over the questions and exercises and your responses to them. Do you need to do something differently? Also look at your affirmative prayer. Does it need to be changed? Be sure to check yourself on negative thought habits. Are you willing to reevaluate your approach and try again?

_____

_____

_____

■ What is the most important thing you have learned about yourself in regard to friendship?

_____

_____

_____

125

REALIZATION

Realization is the third stage of affirmative prayer. In this stage, already knowing you are part of God, you realize without doubt or reservation that the good you desire to experience is now taking form through God's Power — the activity of the Universal Law of Mind.

Purpose of the Realization stage of affirmative prayer: To state clearly and specifically the affirmative experience you desire to have; to know that as you completely accept the activity of God in your life, as your life, any problem you have will be resolved.

Suggestions for creating an effective statement of realization: A realization statement activates the Universal Law of Mind to create the good you desire, so make your statement as clear and concise as you can; take time to create a statement that expresses exactly what you want to experience. Eliminate any fear that you can't possibly have what you want, or the feeling that you don't deserve what you desire. In your realization statement you must deeply affirm that the good you are seeking is already yours right now. See the result happening, feel yourself experiencing this good, and know that you totally accept the result you desire.

When you are ready to write your realization statement, do so with simplicity and sincerity. Know you are now directing the activity of the Universal Law of Mind, which responds to your realization in accordance with your level of conviction and acceptance. Remember, your realization statement should contain only what is for your highest good and should never be used with the intention of manipulating another person. Record your statement on the appropriate page of this workbook.

Examples of Realization statements:

☐ *For money:* Money is a Divine idea. Money flows freely to and from me, enabling me to be comfortable, prosperous, and to enjoy life. God withholds no good thing from me. Money is a symbol of God's ever-flowing Abundance, and I accept that which is rightfully mine.

☐ *For employment:* I now have the perfect position for me. I accept the activity of God which places me in it. I am engaged in work that I fully enjoy, am paid well for, and through which I make a valuable contribution to my world.

☐ *For health:* My body is a creation of God and I affirm that the activity of every cell and organ of my body is harmonious. I accept my Divine wholeness, knowing that the ever available energy, power, and vitality of the universe are freely expressing through me now.

GROWING OLDER

Enter into the spirit of Life, into the joy of living and into the usefulness of being alive. For no one will grow tired and old if he has faith and enthusiasm.
— Ernest Holmes

Whether you're approaching thirty or have passed seventy or eighty, you are experiencing — along with everyone else — both the joys and the frustrations of growing older.

You've had successes and failures. You've gained wisdom, understanding, and compassion and you've known hurt and disappointment. You were involved earlier in life with such matters as getting an education, learning a job or studying for a profession, raising children, and achieving financial security. But now you are moving into a different stage of life and your needs and concerns are different.

While grateful for the good things you've experienced, you may also feel worried about what the future holds. For example, you may fear that opportunities to advance in your job will decrease, your health will decline, you will become less attractive, or you won't have the financial resources you need. If you are having difficulty dealing with these or any other issues that arise as you grow older, remember that you do not need to accept anything less than complete happiness, abundance, and success. As a Divine being, you are unified with all the good of God, and you can experience a life rich in joy and wisdom.

The Presence and Power of God are eternally within you, no matter what your age. So be excited about what is in store for you. Don't be influenced by negative views of growing older. Instead, choose what you want to experience and use affirmative prayer to reveal the Divine qualities of Joy and Wisdom in your life.

As a spiritual being, you are ageless. Believe in your own Divinity. You have the ability, through your conscious, positive use of the Universal Law of Mind, to create a happy, vibrant life. Each day and year can bring as much joy and wisdom as you believe in and accept for yourself. Remember, every moment you have the opportunity to make your life more rewarding.

OLD PATTERNS — NEW POSSIBILITIES

Old Patterns

Your beliefs — which include your thoughts, feelings, and attitudes, both conscious and subconscious — determine what you are now experiencing, for the Universal Law of Mind acts on them to create the circumstances of your life. Use the following exercises to help you become aware of the particular beliefs that underlie your concern about growing older. Take as much time as you need, perhaps a few days, to respond to these questions since they form an important foundation for the work you will be doing to resolve this concern.

■ Look back at "Where Am I Now?" on the subject of growing older (page 22). If you haven't completed that exercise, please do so now. Use the space provided below to answer the following questions: What issues did you respond to with a number 3, 4, or 5? Are these issues related? If so, in what way? Select one of them to work with in this section and note it below.

■ Write down the feelings, especially the fears, you have in regard to this issue. What beliefs can you identify about yourself or about other people that underlie these feelings?

■ What new understanding has come to you as a result of exploring these old belief patterns? On the basis of your new understanding, what would you like to change?

_____

_____

_____

_____

_____

_____

_____

_____

New Possibilities

To break up old patterns of thought and behavior, you need to open yourself to new possibilities. The exercise on the following page, based on contrasting statements, will assist you with this process. Saying the statement in the left column first and then saying the statement in the right column will help you become aware of how you think, break up habitual non-productive patterns of thinking, and expand your consciousness. (Create your own statements if the examples provided do not address your situation.)

When you affirm the statements in either the left or the right column, you are directing the activity of the Universal Law of Mind, which creates your experiences according to the patterns of your thoughts, feelings, and attitudes . . . your beliefs. If these beliefs are consistently negative, your experiences will be negative. If these beliefs are positive, your experiences will be positive. Remember, the Universal Law of Mind does not make choices — *you* make the choices through what you believe. *This means you can consciously choose how to direct the Universal Law of Mind to create the results you want.*

You will be working with these consciousness-expanders as a way of preparing for the next section, "Creating My New Life," in which you use affirmative prayer to deal with your specific concern with growing older. As you read each statement in the right column, see it as a new possibility. Imagine yourself being, acting, and feeling what it expresses. Believe it! Feel the feelings you would have if this statement were actually true right now. In this way you begin the process of changing your thinking.

How do you talk to yourself about your concern? How do you talk to others about it?

If you have been saying:

Now begin to say:

If you have been saying:	Now begin to say:
The older I am the slower I am.	I'm as active as I choose to be.
Younger people get all the promotions.	I have the promotion I deserve.
Growing older scares me.	Each year is more fulfilling.
I feel so alone. Most of my friends have moved away or passed on.	I fill my life with new activities and friends.
Life seems empty with the children gone.	I have new interests to fill my time.
My body feels weak and stiff.	My body is strong and flexible.
I'm not ready for retirement.	I have exciting plans for retirement.
I can't live on just Social Security.	I have additional sources of income.
Remarriage is impossible at my age.	I have a wonderful new spouse.
Growing older is depressing.	Each day is joyful and inspiring.
Men like women younger than I am.	Men find me interesting and attractive.
I'm not as sexually capable as I was.	I'm energetic and vigorous.
I'm afraid I'll be like my parents as I grow older.	I'm an individual, expressing in my own way.
If I'm laid off I'll never get a job.	A better job is always available to me.
I don't want to be dependent on anyone.	I accept help when I need it.
There's so little time to do all I want.	I accomplish everything I want to do.
I'm not as attractive as I used to be.	My attractiveness comes from within me.
No one will take care of me in my old age.	I always have everything I need.
My body is in bad shape.	I stay in shape with diet and exercise.
I don't like how younger people treat me.	Younger people enjoy being with me.

Other_____
(use additional paper if necessary)

_____

Now turn to the next section, "Creating My New Life," to learn to use affirmative prayer to deal with your specific concern about growing older.

DAILY AFFIRMATION:

I now experience more joy and wisdom in my life.

CREATING MY NEW LIFE

In the previous section you started to see that the Universal Law of Mind acts on your beliefs to create your experiences. You began to identify and break free from negative patterns of belief and you are now aware of new possibilities. *Incorporating any additional understanding you gained in that section, write here what you want your new experience to be.*

_____

_____

_____

_____

This portion of the workbook will help you learn how to create an affirmative prayer to resolve your concern about growing older. In affirmative prayer, you align your thinking with the Divine qualities of Joy and Wisdom already inherent within you. When you do this, your experience changes. This change occurs as the Universal Law of Mind acts on your deeply held beliefs. (Remember, when we say "beliefs" we mean thoughts, feelings, and attitudes, both conscious and subconscious.)

Realizing through affirmative prayer that Joy and Wisdom are the truth about God and that you are unified with God, you come to know that joy and wisdom are also the truth about you in regard to growing older. As a result, problems are resolved.

Each of the following exercises has two parts. The first part consists of an activity which helps prepare you to write your affirmative prayer. This activity is designed to assist you in developing an inner atmosphere of strong feeling and conviction, one that will make your statements effective. The second part involves actually writing the five stages of your affirmative prayer. Through this process, as you align your thinking with what is true about God, a solution to your concern about growing older unfolds.

Each of the five stages of affirmative prayer — Recognition, Unification, Realization, Thanksgiving, and Release — is explained fully on the following pages: page 70 (Recognition), page 98 (Unification), page 126 (Realization), page 154 (Thanksgiving), and page 182 (Release). Examples are also provided. Be sure to refer to these examples for guidance and suggestions.

1 Present in all that exists is the fullness of God's infinite and eternal Life. Everywhere you look, observe this perfect Presence expressing as a seed, a sapling, a full-grown tree. Also observe it fully present in the blossoming of spring as well as in the dormancy of winter. Recognizing evidence of the Divine qualities of Joy and Wisdom everywhere, become aware of the creative activity of God's Power in the world around you. Write in the space below what you think and feel about this Presence and Power.

There is a Presence and Power greater than you are — God — which is the Source and the Creator of everything around you. Recognize that there is one God, one Life, one Mind and that it is ever present, ever active, and constantly creative. Now state what you have recognized, letting your statement be as sincere and meaningful as you can.

(See page 70 for examples of Recognition statements.)

2 As you observe the Presence and Power of God everywhere around you, begin now to experience your deep connection with God. Know you are part of God. Know there is one Life, that Life is God, and that Life is what you are. Know there is one Universal Law of Mind which always responds to your beliefs. Feel your oneness with the Divine qualities of Joy and Wisdom, taking time to sense the presence of these qualities within you. When have you experienced joy? When have you sensed an inner wisdom? Remember these occasions and reflect on them. Become still and know that as a spiritual being you are not separate from God-Life, nor are you separate from the Power that gives form to Divine qualities. Write in the space below what this experience of unification feels like.

_____

_____

_____

_____

_____

_____

_____

_____

_____

Observing the Presence and the Power of God everywhere around you, become aware that you are part of a great Unity. Accept and feel your oneness with God. Make a statement below expressing how you experience your oneness with this Presence and Power greater than you are.

_____

_____

_____

_____

_____

(See page 98 for examples of Unification statements.)

3 Maintaining a sense of your unity with a Presence and Power greater than you are, know that Joy and Wisdom exist in place of your concern about growing older. Contemplate this idea, ridding yourself of all doubt or reservation. Become deeply convinced that the new and positive experience you desire is unfolding for you. Record here the feelings you have as you do this.

_____

_____

_____

_____

_____

_____

_____

_____

_____

_____

_____

Make a positive statement of your changed belief. Write it in the present tense, recognizing and accepting the presence of the Divine qualities of Joy and Wisdom where your problem appears to be. You are creating a mold for the Universal Law of Mind, so be clear, definite, and specific. Be emphatic! Imagine that what you desire to experience is now established, knowing that it is already taking form in your life through the activity of the Universal Law of Mind. State here what you are now declaring to be true in place of your concern.

_____

_____

_____

_____

(See page 126 for examples of Realization statements.)

4 Recall an occasion in your life when you felt a great outpouring of gratitude — whether for something specific or simply for the joy of being alive. Recapture in your imagination this special time of feeling grateful, and allow the experience to be fresh and vivid for you again. Describe here the feelings you have.

When you have an attitude of thanksgiving, knowing your need is already met, something in this attitude enhances your ability to have faith and to be open and receptive. Right now, completely and wholeheartedly accept that your concern about growing older is resolved and feel thankful for this solution. Write a statement here expressing your gratitude.

(See page 154 for examples of Thanksgiving statements.)

5 Have you ever had the experience of feeling completely unburdened, as if a great weight had been lifted from your shoulders? What you felt was a letting go, a release. This is what you need to experience in regard to your concern about growing older. Know that the Universal Law of Mind is now creating what you desire. Relax and experience a sense of trust, certain that this resolution is now unfolding. Write below what the experience of release feels like.

Sometimes you may tend to doubt or deny the good you want to experience. The act of releasing your affirmative prayer helps prevent that. When you release it, the Universal Law of Mind can freely respond to your new spiritual understanding, revealing Joy and Wisdom in place of your concern. Right now release all fear and worry, and allow this process to move forward. Let go of the problem and be confident that the good you desire is already unfolding. Write a statement releasing your affirmative prayer to the activity of the Universal Law of Mind.

(See page 182 for examples of Release statements.)

MY AFFIRMATIVE PRAYER

Taken together, the statements you have made at the bottom of the previous five pages comprise a complete affirmative prayer, addressing the particular concern about growing older you have chosen to deal with. This prayer consists of the stages of Recognition, Unification, Realization, Thanksgiving, and Release.

Review each of your five statements now and determine if there are any changes you wish to make in them. As you review them, be sure they evoke deep feeling and conviction in you and are worded concisely for maximum impact. Also be sure they achieve the purpose intended. For example, when you reread your Realization statement, are you able to sense the Joy and Wisdom of God in your life? After you make any desired changes in your five statements, combine them below into a complete unit.

1 Recognition:

2 Unification:

3 Realization:

4 Thanksgiving:

5 Release:

WHERE DO I GO FROM HERE?

You have now started a process of personal and spiritual growth that will produce new and positive changes for you.

You can do several things to continue the work you started in this section. Stay alert to the statements you make about your situation. At night recall your habitual thought patterns of the day. How much of your thinking was negative and how much was positive? Practice changing the negative statements into positive ones. Say the positive statements over and over until you begin to feel a definite connection with them.

Most important, read your affirmative prayer several times a day. At a minimum, we suggest doing so right before going to bed and upon waking in the morning. Read it out loud if possible. Take time to contemplate it. As you read your prayer and think about it, experience the feelings associated with each of the five stages. Be sure to make reading it meaningful, not simply an automatic exercise. If one of your statements seems to lose impact for you, redo it.

Remain open to change and be willing to follow any inner guidance that comes to you. God works in your life through such inner guidance, which often appears as a new idea or an urge to do something differently. As you allow change to occur, what was originally a problem will be replaced by more desirable circumstances. Remain open-minded and patient, knowing that positive results are certain to take place.

Remember, there is a natural process by which spiritual truth takes form, and the time this process requires varies with different situations. You may have an immediate response to your affirmative prayer or a period of weeks or even months may elapse, but continue with your affirmative prayer, always using the present tense, accepting that what you desire *is now happening*. Keep deepening your level of conviction and adjust the wording of your prayer to reflect your changed state of consciousness. Feel free to create new affirmations and affirmative prayers as your understanding of your unity with God's Joy and Wisdom expands. Continue with your affirmative prayer until the desired result is obtained.

HOW AM I CHANGING?

Work with the "Old Patterns — New Possibilities" and "Creating My New Life" sections for two to three weeks, then respond to these questions. They will help you assess your progress and guide you if you need assistance. (Since keeping a record of your experiences is useful when you are seeking to improve your life, you may also want to write your continuing insights in a separate notebook.)

■ What changes have you experienced in your situation as a result of working with this section on growing older?

_____

_____

_____

_____

■ Are you satisfied with these results? If you are, what do you think is responsible for your improved circumstances?

_____

_____

_____

_____

■ If you feel you are not making progress, go back over the questions and exercises and your responses to them. Do you need to do something differently? Also look at your affirmative prayer. Does it need to be changed? Be sure to check yourself on negative thought habits. Are you willing to reevaluate your approach and try again?

_____

_____

_____

_____

■ What is the most important thing you have learned about yourself in regard to growing older?

_____

_____

_____

ADDICTION

The truth about my real Self reveals to my mind a complete freedom from any habit that could rob me of peace or of my rightful mentality.
— Ernest Holmes

Addiction is a way of hiding from feelings. The addict retreats from life, becoming dependent on a substance, an activity, or a person to help dull pain and ease feelings of fear. Thus addictive behavior is not limited to the use of illegal drugs. It can involve such everyday pursuits as working, exercising, watching television, shopping, or reading, if they are engaged in as a substitute for living and feeling. It can also include an obsessive attachment to a particular person in your life. Other common addictions involve the excessive use of coffee, cigarettes, prescribed medication, and alcohol.

Often what causes addictive behavior are unconscious feelings of shame, guilt, or unworthiness, which lead to negative beliefs about yourself. The following exercises help you explore these beliefs and also guide you in replacing them with others that are positive and self-affirming. Recognizing your unity with the Presence and Power of God, you will become aware that the Freedom and Strength of God are within you. Then, as the Universal Law of Mind acts on this new awareness, you will discover greater freedom and inner strength in your life.

Completing this process may take a long time, but the fundamental changes can begin immediately. Day by day you will discover in yourself strength, courage, self-confidence, and enthusiasm. And life won't seem to be happening capriciously to you. Rather, you will feel in command of your circumstances and equal to the challenges you are called upon to meet.

Be willing to look within yourself and explore the fears and beliefs which have held you in bondage. Then set about to change them — for you can! Replace them with a new awareness of your unity with the Presence and Power of God. Begin to know that as a spiritual being you are blessed with wondrous gifts, then accept these gifts. Enjoy a new life, free from dependency, and know the peace and fulfillment of expressing who you truly are.

OLD PATTERNS — NEW POSSIBILITIES

Old Patterns

Your beliefs — which include your thoughts, feelings, and attitudes, both conscious and subconscious — determine what you are now experiencing, for the Universal Law of Mind acts on them to create the circumstances of your life. Use the following exercises to help you become aware of the particular beliefs that underlie your concern about addiction. Take as much time as you need, perhaps a few days, to respond to these questions since they form an important foundation for the work you will be doing to resolve your concern.

■ Look back at "Where Am I Now?" on the subject of addiction (page 23). If you haven't completed that exercise, please do so now. Use the space provided below to answer the following questions: What issues did you respond to with a number 3, 4, or 5? Are these issues related? If so, in what way? Select one of them to work with in this section and note it below.

_____

_____

_____

_____

_____

_____

_____

■ Write down the feelings, especially the fears, you have in regard to this issue. What beliefs can you identify about yourself or about other people that underlie these feelings?

_____

_____

_____

_____

_____

_____

■ What new understanding has come to you as a result of exploring these old belief patterns? On the basis of your new understanding, what would you like to change?

_____

_____

_____

_____

_____

_____

_____

_____

New Possibilities

To break up old patterns of thought and behavior, you need to open yourself to new possibilities. The exercise on the following page, based on contrasting statements, will assist you with this process. Saying the statement in the left column first and then saying the statement in the right column will help you become aware of how you think, and also help you break up habitual non-productive patterns of thinking and expand your consciousness. (Create your own statements if the examples provided do not address your situation.)

When you affirm the statements in either the left or the right column, you are directing the activity of the Universal Law of Mind, which creates your experiences according to the patterns of your thoughts, feelings, and attitudes . . . your beliefs. If these beliefs are consistently negative, your experiences will be negative. If these beliefs are positive, your experiences will be positive. Remember, the Universal Law of Mind does not make choices — *you* make the choices through what you believe. *This means you can consciously choose how to direct the Universal Law of Mind to create the results you want.*

You will be working with these consciousness-expanders as a way of preparing for the next section, "Creating My New Life," in which you use affirmative prayer to deal with your specific concern with addiction. As you read each statement in the right column, see it as a new possibility. Imagine yourself being, acting, and feeling what it expresses. Believe it! Feel the feelings you would have if this statement were actually true right now. In this way you begin the process of changing your thinking.

How do you talk to yourself about your problem? How do you talk to others about it?

If you have been saying:	Now begin to say:
I need my tranquilizers.	**I am calm without tranquilizers.**
I'm hooked on cocaine.	**I am free of cocaine.**
I can't control my eating.	**I eat balanced, nutritious meals.**
When things get tough, I drink.	**I handle stress without drinking.**
I'm gambling too much.	**My need to gamble is gone.**
I can't stop smoking.	**I have successfully stopped smoking.**
I watch TV to escape from things I don't want to do.	**I take care of what needs to be done before watching TV.**
I can't take time off.	**I relax and delegate work to others.**
I stuff myself with junk food.	**I love myself and eat healthful food.**
I need to have everything perfect.	**I quit judging myself.**
I can't leave this abusive relationship.	**I am in control of my life.**
I must have several cups of coffee a day.	Life is stimulating without coffee.
My credit card use is out of control.	**I control my use of credit cards.**
I can't relax until everything is clean.	**I relax without finishing everything.**
I smoke too much pot.	**I don't need to smoke pot.**
I can't sleep without pills.	**I sleep well without drugs.**
I'm addicted to daytime soap operas.	I love real life more than soaps.
I need a few drinks to relax.	I no longer need alcohol in my life.
I can't get thin enough.	I treat my body with respect.
I haven't taken a vacation in years.	I balance work with play.

Other_____   _____
(use additional paper if necessary)

Now turn to the next section, "Creating My New Life," to learn to use affirmative prayer to deal with your specific addiction problem.

DAILY AFFIRMATION:

I feel strong and whole within myself and I am free from all addiction.

CREATING MY NEW LIFE

In the previous section you started to see that the Universal Law of Mind acts on your beliefs to create your experiences. You began to identify and break free from negative patterns of belief and you are now aware of new possibilities. *Incorporating any additional understanding you gained in that section, write here what you want your new experience to be.*

This portion of the workbook will help you learn how to create an affirmative prayer to resolve your concern with addiction. In affirmative prayer, you align your thinking with the Divine qualities of Freedom and Strength already inherent within you. When you do this, your experience changes. This change occurs as the Universal Law of Mind acts on your new beliefs. (Remember, when we say "beliefs" we mean thoughts, feelings, and attitudes, both conscious and subconscious.)

Realizing through affirmative prayer that Freedom and Strength are the truth about God and that you are unified with God, you come to know that freedom and strength are also the truth about you in regard to addiction. As a result, problems are resolved.

Each of the following exercises has two parts. The first part consists of an activity which helps prepare you to write your affirmative prayer. This activity is designed to assist you in developing an inner atmosphere of strong feeling and conviction, one that will make your statements effective. The second part involves actually writing the five stages of your affirmative prayer. Through this process, as you align your thinking with what is true about God, a solution to your concern with addiction unfolds.

Each of the five stages of affirmative prayer — Recognition, Unification, Realization, Thanksgiving, and Release — is explained fully on the following pages: page 70 (Recognition), page 98 (Unification), page 126 (Realization), page 154 (Thanksgiving), and page 182 (Release). Examples are also provided. Be sure to refer to these examples for guidance and suggestions.

▮ An infinite Presence and Power exists in the world. Observe this perfect Life around you in the free unfolding of all of nature's processes — the unrestricted flow of water, the effortless blossoming of a flower, the lush growth of greenery after a rainfall. Also observe the strength evident in nature, a strength that can carve canyons and raise mountains. Recognizing the Divine qualities of Freedom and Strength everywhere, become aware of the creative activity of God's Power in the world around you. Write in the space below what you think and feel about this Presence and Power.

There is a Presence and Power greater than you are — God — which is the Source and the Creator of everything around you. Recognize that there is one God, one Life, one Mind and that it is ever present, ever active, and constantly creative. Now state what you have recognized, letting your statement be as sincere and meaningful as you can.

(See page 70 for examples of Recognition statements.)

2 As you observe the Presence and Power of God everywhere around you, begin to experience your deep connection with God. Know you are part of God. Know there is one Life, that Life is God, and that Life is what you are. Know there is one Universal Law of Mind which always responds to your beliefs. Feel your oneness with the Divine qualities of Freedom and Strength, taking time to sense the presence of these qualities within you. When have you felt strong and free? Remember these occasions and reflect on them. Become still and know that as a spiritual being you are not separate from God-Life, nor are you separate from the Power that gives form to Divine qualities. Write in the space below what this experience of unification feels like.

Observing the Presence and the Power of God everywhere around you, become aware that you are part of a great Unity. Accept and feel your oneness with God. Make a statement below expressing how you experience your oneness with this Presence and Power greater than you are.

(See page 98 for examples of Unification statements.)

3 Maintaining a sense of your unity with a Presence and Power greater than you are, know that Freedom and Strength exist in place of your concern with addiction. Contemplate this idea, ridding yourself of all doubt or reservation. Become deeply convinced that the new and positive experience you desire is unfolding for you. Record here the feelings you have as you do this.

Make a positive statement of your changed belief. Write it in the present tense, recognizing and accepting the presence of the Divine qualities of Freedom and Strength where your problem appears to be. You are creating a mold for the Universal Law of Mind, so be clear, definite, and specific. Be emphatic! Imagine that what you desire to experience is now established, knowing that it is already taking form in your life through the activity of the Universal Law of Mind. State here what you are now declaring to be true in place of your problem.

(See page 126 for examples of Realization statements.)

4 Recall an occasion in your life when you felt a great outpouring of gratitude — whether for something specific or simply for the joy of being alive. Recapture in your imagination this special time of feeling grateful, and allow the experience to be fresh and vivid for you again. Describe here the feelings you have.

When you have an attitude of thanksgiving, knowing your need is already met, something in this attitude enhances your ability to have faith and to be open and receptive. Right now, completely and wholeheartedly accept that the problem you have with addiction is resolved and feel thankful for this solution. Write a statement here expressing your gratitude.

(See page 154 for examples of Thanksgiving statements.)

5 Have you ever had the experience of feeling completely unburdened, as if a great weight had been lifted from your shoulders? What you felt was a letting go, a release. This is what you need to experience in regard to your problem with addiction. Know that the Universal Law of Mind is now creating what you desire. Relax and experience a sense of trust, certain that this resolution is unfolding. Write below what the experience of release feels like.

Sometimes you may tend to doubt or deny the good you want to experience. The act of releasing your affirmative prayer helps prevent that. When you release it, the Universal Law of Mind can freely respond to your new spiritual understanding, revealing Freedom and Strength in place of your problem. Right now release all fear and worry, and allow this process to move forward. Let go of the problem and be confident that the good you desire is already unfolding. Write a statement releasing your affirmative prayer to the activity of the Universal Law of Mind.

(See page 182 for examples of Release statements.)

MY AFFIRMATIVE PRAYER

Taken together, the statements you have made at the bottom of the previous five pages comprise a complete affirmative prayer, addressing the particular concern about addiction you have chosen to deal with. This prayer consists of the stages of Recognition, Unification, Realization, Thanksgiving, and Release.

Review each of your five statements now and determine if there are any changes you wish to make in them. As you review them, be sure they evoke deep feeling and conviction in you and are worded concisely for maximum impact. Also be sure they achieve the purpose intended. For example, when you reread your Realization statement, are you able to sense the Freedom and Strength of God in your life? After you make any desired changes in your five statements, combine them below into a complete unit.

1 Recognition: _____

_____

_____

2 Unification: _____

_____

_____

_____

3 Realization: _____

_____

_____

_____

4 Thanksgiving: _____

_____

_____

_____

5 Release: _____

_____

_____

WHERE DO I GO FROM HERE?

You have now started a process of personal and spiritual growth that will produce new and positive changes for you.

You can do several things to continue the work you started in this section. Stay alert to the statements you make about your situation. At night recall your habitual thought patterns of the day. How much of your thinking was negative and how much was positive? Practice changing the negative statements into positive ones. Say the positive statements over and over until you begin to feel a definite connection with them.

Most important, read your affirmative prayer several times a day. At a minimum, we suggest doing so right before going to bed and upon waking in the morning. Read it out loud if possible. Take time to contemplate it. As you read your prayer and think about it, experience the feelings associated with each of the five stages. Be sure to make reading it meaningful, not simply an automatic exercise. If one of your statements seems to lose impact for you, redo it.

Remain open to change and be willing to follow any inner guidance that comes to you. God works in your life through such inner guidance, which often appears as a new idea or an urge to do something differently. As you allow change to occur, what was originally a problem will be replaced by more desirable circumstances. Remain open-minded and patient, knowing that positive results are certain to take place.

Remember, there is a natural process by which spiritual truth takes form, and the time this process requires varies with different situations. You may have an immediate response to your affirmative prayer or a period of weeks or even months may elapse, but continue with your affirmative prayer, always using the present tense, accepting that what you desire *is now happening*. Keep deepening your level of conviction and adjust the wording of your prayer to reflect your changed state of consciousness. Feel free to create new affirmations and affirmative prayers as your understanding of your unity with God's Freedom and Strength expands. Continue with your affirmative prayer until the desired result is obtained.

HOW AM I CHANGING?

Work with the "Old Patterns — New Possibilities" and "Creating My New Life" sections for two to three weeks, then respond to these questions. They will help you assess your progress and guide you if you need assistance. (Since keeping a record of your experiences is useful when you are seeking to improve your life, you may also want to write your continuing insights in a separate notebook.)

■ What changes have you experienced in your situation as a result of working with this section on addiction?

_____

_____

_____

_____

■ Are you satisfied with these results? If you are, what do you think is responsible for your improved circumstances?

_____

_____

_____

_____

■ If you feel you are not making progress, go back over the questions and exercises and your responses to them. Do you need to do something differently? Also look at your affirmative prayer. Does it need to be changed? Be sure to check yourself on negative thought habits. Are you willing to reevaluate your approach and try again?

_____

_____

_____

_____

■ What is the most important thing you have learned about yourself in regard to addiction?

_____

_____

_____

_____

THANKSGIVING

Thanksgiving is the fourth stage of affirmative prayer. In this stage, having clearly stated what you want to experience, you thankfully accept that the good you desire is yours right now.

Purpose of the Thanksgiving stage of affirmative prayer: To express gratitude that your affirmative prayer is already answered; to help you accept the fulfillment of your desire as accomplished now.

Suggestions for creating an effective statement of thanksgiving: A statement of thanksgiving expresses how you feel about receiving the good you have directed the Universal Law of Mind to create. First look at your attitude toward receiving. Do you have difficulty receiving gifts or accepting acts of kindness from other people? Let go of any feelings of unworthiness and know you are worthy to receive the good you have claimed in your realization statement. Create a statement of thanksgiving that expresses your appreciation for the response of the Universal Law of Mind. In doing this, you are opening yourself to a deeper knowing of the activity of God in your life. Be sure to state that you accept the fulfillment of your desire now, not at some future time.

Let your heart be filled with thanksgiving that you are now experiencing what you desire. Then write the words that come from this feeling of gratitude. Enjoy this wonderful feeling of knowing that something has been accomplished. Record your statement on the appropriate page of this workbook.

Examples of Thanksgiving statements:

☐ I accept that harmony is established in my life now through the action of the Universal Law of Mind. I am deeply grateful for this and for every life-enhancing activity I experience, knowing that as I identify myself with the Divine Presence, my life is always filled with that which represents my highest good.

☐ As I state my words of thanksgiving, I experience perfect faith in God and acceptance of my good. With gratitude I realize my oneness with the Divine Presence and Power. I know that no good I seek is denied me. I am one with the Life of God.

☐ With joy I acknowledge the perfect fulfillment of my desire. I know it has been established by the Universal Law of Mind and for this I do give thanks. Every day I am deeply grateful for the beauty, the joy, and the abundance I experience.

DEATH AND DYING

What we call death is only an expansion of the soul, an enlargement of experience, a gateway into higher expressions of life and truth.
— Ernest Holmes

Death is a subject you may not like to think about. Most people don't. When you do think about it — whether you are dealing with the death of someone close to you or contemplating your own eventual death — you may experience the painful emotions of fear, anger, sorrow, or grief. At such times, using affirmative prayer to recognize that you are unified with the Presence and Power of God eases these feelings and helps you view death as a transition into a new and more expanded life expression.

Perhaps you don't fear death itself but rather you are afraid of dying and the discomfort you believe may accompany it. If you are experiencing this, use affirmative prayer to help you deal with your fear, and align yourself with the abiding presence of the Peace and Comfort of God in your life. The Universal Law of Mind responds to your awareness of these qualities within yourself, and you begin to experience peace and comfort in place of your fear of dying.

You are a spiritual being clothed in a physical body, a body which serves a specific purpose in this life. Your spiritual essence can never be destroyed. You are immortal right now, and death is not an end to life but simply a change of form. As a spiritual being you are ever evolving into a greater awareness of your unity with God, the Creator as well as the Essence of all life. At some future point your body will no longer be necessary to this evolving process and you will leave it through death.

As you work with the following exercises, explore any feelings of anxiety, fear, anger, guilt, or sadness you have in regard to death or dying. Use affirmative prayer to address the particular problem with death or dying you now face and free yourself to move peacefully forward into the future. Viewing death as part of the larger life, remain open to living as fully as possible, now and always.

OLD PATTERNS — NEW POSSIBILITIES

Old Patterns

Your beliefs — which include your thoughts, feelings, and attitudes, both conscious and subconscious — determine what you are now experiencing, for the Universal Law of Mind acts on them to create the circumstances of your life. Use the following exercises to help you become aware of the particular beliefs that underlie your concern about death or dying. Take as much time as you need, perhaps a few days, to respond to these questions since they form an important foundation for the work you will be doing to resolve your concern.

■ Look back at "Where Am I Now?" on the subject of death and dying (page 24). If you haven't completed that exercise, please do so now. Use the space provided below to answer the following questions: What issues did you respond to with a number 3, 4, or 5? Are these issues related? If so, in what way? Select one of them to work with in this section and note it below.

_____

_____

_____

_____

_____

_____

■ Write down the feelings, especially the fears, you have in regard to this issue. What beliefs can you identify about yourself or about other people that underlie these feelings?

_____

_____

_____

_____

_____

_____

_____

_____

■ What new understanding has come to you as a result of exploring these old belief patterns? On the basis of your new understanding, what would you like to change?

_____

_____

_____

_____

_____

_____

_____

New Possibilities

To break up old patterns of thought and behavior, you need to open yourself to new possibilities. The exercise on the following page, based on contrasting statements, will assist you with this process. Saying the statement in the left column first and then saying the statement in the right column will help you become aware of how you think, and also help you break up habitual non-productive patterns of thinking and expand your consciousness. (Create your own statements if the examples provided do not address your situation.)

When you affirm the statements in either the left or the right column, you are directing the activity of the Universal Law of Mind, which creates your experiences according to the patterns of your thoughts, feelings, and attitudes . . . your beliefs. If these beliefs are consistently negative, your experiences will be negative. If these beliefs are positive, your experiences will be positive. Remember, the Universal Law of Mind does not make choices — *you* make the choices through what you believe. *This means you can consciously choose how to direct the Universal Law of Mind to create the results you want.*

You will be working with these consciousness-expanders as a way of preparing for the next section, "Creating My New Life," in which you use affirmative prayer to deal with your specific concern with death or dying. As you read the statement in the right column, see it as a new possibility. Imagine yourself being, acting, and feeling what it expresses. Believe it! Feel the feelings you would have if this statement were actually true right now. In this way you begin the process of changing your thinking.

How do you talk to yourself about your concern? How do you talk to others about it?

If you have been saying:	Now begin to say:
I'm afraid of a painful death.	I will experience a death without pain.
I'm concerned that I'll no longer exist.	I am eternal. I will always exist.
I'm angry when someone I love dies.	I acknowledge my anger and deal with it.
I don't want to talk about dying.	I can freely talk about dying.
I'm worried about medical costs.	My medical costs are totally covered.
I don't want to die.	I look beyond death to a new life.
I don't want to be a burden to others.	I am never a burden to others.
My spouse shouldn't have died first.	I lovingly accept my spouse's death.
I'm concerned about leaving my children.	I prepare my loved ones for my absence.
Why do I have to die while others live?	Each person's life is unique.
I wish I'd told my parents I loved them before they died.	In quiet contemplation I express my feelings of love.
I'd like to have accomplished more.	I am pleased with what I have done.
I'm scared about what happens after death.	I believe in an eternal, expanding life.
My financial affairs are in a mess.	I take care of my will and finances.
I'll always feel guilty about some things.	I forgive myself and release all guilt.
I'm afraid of eternal punishment.	God is Love. Love is eternal.
I am overwhelmed by grief.	Knowing time heals, I let myself grieve.
I fear God's judgment after death.	God is Love. God does not judge.
I have unfinished business with people.	I am complete with everyone.
I wish I'd had more fun.	I take time now to enjoy life.

Other_____   _____
(use additional paper if necessary)

Now turn to the next section, "Creating My New Life," to learn to use affirmative prayer to deal with your specific issue relating to death or dying.

DAILY AFFIRMATION:

My new understanding of life brings me comfort and peace.

CREATING MY NEW LIFE

In the previous section you started to see that the Universal Law of Mind acts on your beliefs to create your experiences. You began to identify and break free from negative patterns of belief and you are now aware of new possibilities. *Incorporating any additional understanding you gained in that section, write here what you want your new experience to be.*

_____

_____

_____

_____

This portion of the workbook will help you learn how to create an affirmative prayer to resolve your concern about death or dying. In affirmative prayer, you align your thinking with the Divine qualities of Peace and Comfort already inherent within you. When you do this, your experience changes. This change occurs as the Universal Law of Mind acts on your new beliefs. (Remember, when we say "beliefs" we mean thoughts, feelings, and attitudes, both conscious and subconscious.)

Realizing through affirmative prayer that Peace and Comfort are the truth about God and that you are unified with God, you come to know that peace and comfort are also the truth about you in regard to death or dying. As a result, problems are resolved.

Each of the following exercises has two parts. The first part consists of an activity which helps prepare you to write your affirmative prayer. This activity is designed to assist you in developing an inner atmosphere of strong feeling and conviction, one that will make your statements effective. The second part involves actually writing the five stages of your affirmative prayer. Through this process, as you align your thinking with what is true about God, a solution to your concern with death or dying unfolds.

Each of the five stages of affirmative prayer — Recognition, Unification, Realization, Thanksgiving, and Release — is explained fully on the following pages: page 70 (Recognition), page 98 (Unification), page 126 (Realization), page 154 (Thanksgiving), and page 182 (Release). Examples are also provided. Be sure to refer to these examples for guidance and suggestions.

■ There exists a Presence and Power in the universe which forever endures. Notice in nature how winter's appearance of death gives way to flourishing new growth in the spring, and observe evidence of the eternal Life of God in this seasonal change. Become aware that the perfect Life of God is never altered, depleted, or exhausted and that continuity is the truth of all of creation. Recognizing the existence of the abiding presence of Divine Peace and Comfort in the midst of flux and change, become aware of the activity of God's Power in the world around you. Write in the space below what you think and feel about this Presence and Power.

There is a Presence and Power greater than you are — God — which is the Creator of everything around you. Recognize that there is one God, one Life, one Mind and that it is ever present, ever active, and constantly creative. Now state what you have recognized, letting your statement be as sincere and meaningful as you can.

(See page 70 for examples of Recognition statements.)

2 As you observe the Presence and Power of God everywhere around you, begin now to experience your deep connection with God. Know there is one Life, that Life is God, and that Life is what you are. Know there is one Universal Law of Mind which always responds to your beliefs. Feel your oneness with the Divine qualities of Peace and Comfort, taking time to sense the presence of these qualities within you. When have you felt completely at peace? When have you had a great sense of being comforted? Remember these occasions and reflect on them. Become still and know that as a spiritual being you are not separate from God-Life, nor are you separate from the Power that gives form to Divine qualities. Write in the space below what this experience of unification feels like.

Observing the Presence and the Power of God everywhere around you, become aware that you are part of a great Unity. Accept and feel your oneness with God. Make a statement below expressing how you experience your oneness with this Presence and Power greater than you are.

(See page 98 for examples of Unification statements.)

3 Maintaining a sense of your unity with a Presence and Power greater than you are, know that Peace and Comfort exist in place of your concern with death or dying. Contemplate this idea, ridding yourself of all doubt or reservation. Become deeply convinced that the new and positive experience you desire is unfolding for you. Record here the feelings you have as you do this.

_____

_____

_____

_____

_____

_____

_____

_____

_____

_____

_____

Make a positive statement of your changed belief. Write it in the present tense, recognizing and accepting the presence of the Divine qualities of Peace and Comfort where your concern appears to be. You are creating a mold for the Universal Law of Mind, so be clear, definite, and specific. Be emphatic! Imagine that what you desire to experience is now established, knowing that it is already taking form in your life through the activity of the Universal Law of Mind. State here what you are now declaring to be true in place of your concern in regard to death or dying.

_____

_____

_____

_____

_____

(See page 126 for examples of Realization statements.)

4 Recall an occasion in your life when you felt a great outpouring of gratitude — whether for something specific or simply for the joy of being alive. Recapture in your imagination this special time of feeling grateful, and allow the experience to be fresh and vivid for you again. Describe here the feelings you have.

When you have an attitude of thanksgiving, knowing your need is already met, something in this attitude enhances your ability to have faith and to be open and receptive. Right now, completely and wholeheartedly accept that your concern with death or dying is resolved and feel thankful for this solution. Write a statement here expressing your gratitude.

(See page 154 for examples of Thanksgiving statements.)

5 Have you ever had the experience of feeling completely unburdened, as if a great weight had been lifted from your shoulders? What you felt was a letting go, a release. This is what you need to experience in regard to your concern with death or dying. Know that the Universal Law of Mind is now creating what you desire. Relax and experience a sense of trust, certain that this resolution is unfolding. Write below what the experience of release feels like.

Sometimes you may tend to doubt or deny the good you want to experience. The act of releasing your affirmative prayer helps prevent that. When you release it, the Universal Law of Mind can freely respond to your new spiritual understanding, revealing Peace and Comfort in place of your concern. Right now release all fear and worry, and allow this process to move forward. Let go of your concern and be confident that the good you desire is already unfolding. Write a statement releasing your affirmative prayer to the activity of the Universal Law of Mind.

(See page 182 for examples of Release statements.)

MY AFFIRMATIVE PRAYER

Taken together, the statements you have made at the bottom of the previous five pages comprise a complete affirmative prayer, addressing the particular concern about death or dying you have chosen to deal with. This prayer consists of the stages of Recognition, Unification, Realization, Thanksgiving, and Release.

Review each of your five statements now and determine if there are any changes you wish to make in them. As you review them, be sure they evoke deep feeling and conviction in you and are worded concisely for maximum impact. Also be sure they achieve the purpose intended. For example, when you reread your Realization statement, are you able to sense the Peace and Comfort of God in your life? After you make any desired changes in your five statements, combine them below into a complete unit.

1 Recognition: ....
....
....

2 Unification: ....
....
....

3 Realization: ....
....
....

4 Thanksgiving: ....
....
....

5 Release: ....
....
....

WHERE DO I GO FROM HERE?

You have now started a process of personal and spiritual growth that will produce new and positive changes for you.

You can do several things to continue the work you started in this section. Stay alert to the statements you make about your situation. At night recall your habitual thought patterns of the day. How much of your thinking was negative and how much was positive? Practice changing the negative statements into positive ones. Say the positive statements over and over until you begin to feel a definite connection with them.

Most important, read your affirmative prayer several times a day. At a minimum, we suggest doing so right before going to bed and upon waking in the morning. Read it out loud if possible. Take time to contemplate it. As you read your prayer and think about it, experience the feelings associated with each of the five stages. Be sure to make reading it meaningful, not simply an automatic exercise. If one of your statements seems to lose impact for you, redo it.

Remain open to change and be willing to follow any inner guidance that comes to you. God works in your life through such inner guidance, which often appears as a new idea or an urge to do something differently. As you allow change to occur, what was originally a problem will be replaced by peaceful and comfortable circumstances. Remain open-minded and patient, knowing that the good you desire is certain to take place.

Remember, there is a natural process by which spiritual truth takes form, and the time this process requires varies with different situations. You may have an immediate response to your affirmative prayer or a period of weeks or even months may elapse, but continue with your affirmative prayer, always using the present tense, accepting that what you desire *is now happening*. Keep deepening your level of conviction and adjust the wording of your prayer to reflect your changed state of consciousness. Feel free to create new affirmations and affirmative prayers as your understanding of your unity with God's Peace and Comfort expands. Continue with your affirmative prayer until the desired result is obtained.

HOW AM I CHANGING?

Work with the "Old Patterns — New Possibilities" and "Creating My New Life" sections for two to three weeks, then respond to these questions. They will help you assess your progress and guide you if you need assistance. (Since keeping a record of your experiences is useful when you are seeking to improve your life, you may also want to write your continuing insights in a separate notebook.)

■ What changes have you experienced in your situation as a result of working with this section on death and dying?

_____

_____

_____

■ Are you satisfied with these results? If you are, what do you think is responsible for your improved circumstances?

_____

_____

_____

■ If you feel you are not making progress, go back over the questions and exercises and your responses to them. Do you need to do something differently? Also look at your affirmative prayer. Does it need to be changed? Be sure to check yourself on negative thought habits. Are you willing to reevaluate your approach and try again?

_____

_____

_____

■ What is the most important thing you have learned about yourself in regard to death or dying?

_____

_____

_____

EMOTIONAL WELL-BEING

We must begin to feel that we are already surrounded by happiness just because we are already surrounded by God, the living Spirit. Praying for happiness with this attitude of mind is certain to produce a result if we accept that happiness as being ours right now.
— Ernest Holmes

Emotional well-being involves feeling inwardly at peace, being on harmonious terms with life, and having confidence in your ability to meet the challenges of living. From time to time you may feel hurt, sad, or lonely, but when you have a basic sense of emotional well-being, you are generally free from extreme plunges into such negative emotions as depression, guilt, fear, anxiety, resentment, worry, and hate.

Do you presently feel caught in the grip of these or any other painful emotions? Does your life often seem to be an emotional battleground? If so, there is a solution. Through the use of affirmative prayer, you can begin to experience the peace and serenity you desire. Knowing that the Source of all peace is eternally within you and will never be apart from you is the first step toward a sense of emotional well-being deeper and more lasting than you have ever felt before. As you use affirmative prayer, recognizing your unity with the Peace and Serenity of God, inner turmoil is dissolved. The Universal Law of Mind responds to your inner image of peace, and you become peaceful. You learn to love and forgive yourself and to flow more harmoniously with the stream of life.

Using the exercises on the following pages will help you explore the beliefs that underlie any emotional pain you are now experiencing. Then as you align yourself through affirmative prayer with the Presence and Power of God, you will be able to deal effectively with any distress you are feeling, finding instead a new peace and serenity.

Remember that the life of God is always present within you. All you have to do to experience the Peace and Serenity that flow from God is to recognize your unity with these Divine qualities and accept them as your reality.

OLD PATTERNS — NEW POSSIBILITIES

Old Patterns

Your beliefs — which include your thoughts, feelings, and attitudes, both conscious and subconscious — determine what you are now experiencing, for the Universal Law of Mind acts on them to create the circumstances of your life. Use the following exercises to help you become aware of the particular beliefs that underlie your emotional concern. Take as much time as you need, perhaps a few days, to respond to these questions since they form an important foundation for the work you will be doing to resolve your concern.

■ Look back at "Where Am I Now?" on the subject of emotional well-being (page 25). If you haven't completed that exercise, please do so now. Use the space provided below to answer the following questions: What issues did you respond to with a number 3, 4, or 5? Are these issues related? If so, in what way? Select one of them to work with in this section and note it below.

_____

_____

_____

_____

_____

■ Write down the feelings, especially the fears, you have in regard to this issue. What beliefs can you identify about yourself or about other people that underlie these feelings?

_____

_____

_____

_____

_____

_____

_____

■ What new understanding has come to you as a result of exploring these old belief patterns? On the basis of your new understanding, what would you like to change?

_____

_____

_____

_____

_____

_____

_____

_____

_____

New Possibilities

To break up old patterns of thought and behavior, you need to open yourself to new possibilities. The exercise on the following page, based on contrasting statements, will assist you with this process. Saying the statement in the left column first and then saying the statement in the right column will help you become aware of how you think, and also help you break up habitual non-productive patterns of thinking and expand your consciousness. (Create your own statements if the examples provided do not address your situation.)

When you affirm the statements in either the left or the right column, you are directing the activity of the Universal Law of Mind, which creates your experiences according to the patterns of your thoughts, feelings, and attitudes...your beliefs. If these beliefs are consistently negative, your experiences will be negative. If these beliefs are positive, your experiences will be positive. Remember, the Universal Law of Mind does not make choices — *you* make the choices through what you believe. *This means you can consciously choose how to direct the Universal Law of Mind to create the results you want.*

You will be working with these consciousness-expanders as a way of preparing for the next section, "Creating My New Life," in which you use affirmative prayer to deal with your specific emotional concern. As you read each statement in the right column, see it as a new possibility. Imagine yourself being, acting, and feeling what it expresses. Believe it! Feel the feelings you would have if this statement were actually true right now. In this way you begin the process of changing your thinking.

How do you talk to yourself about your concern? How do you talk to others about it?

If you have been saying:

I am easily frustrated.

I can't help being anxious.

I am afraid to try new things.

I feel intimidated by people.

My quick temper troubles me.

I feel guilty about many past actions.

I am often confused.

I resent many things that happen to me.

I have difficulty asserting myself.

I can't express my feelings.

I feel tense all the time.

I'm a failure.

I feel empty inside.

No one understands me.

I don't feel loved.

I want to escape everything.

I feel powerless much of the time.

My life is very lonely.

I am awfully shy around people.

I worry all the time.

Other_____

(use additional paper if necessary)

Now begin to say:

I meet every situation calmly.

I love myself and release my fears.

I courageously try new things.

I am self-confident with everyone.

I relax and respond calmly to events.

I forgive myself and release all guilt.

I take time to think and act clearly.

I look for the good in each moment.

I confidently express myself.

I clearly express my feelings.

I relax and open myself to life.

I am capable and successful.

My life is filled with love and joy.

I am understood and appreciated.

I love myself and am loved by others.

I enjoy and embrace life fully.

I am secure in who I am.

I see a friend in every person.

I am comfortable with people.

I have faith in myself.

_____

Now turn to the next section, "Creating My New Life," to learn to use affirmative prayer to deal with your specific emotional issue.

DAILY AFFIRMATION:

I let go of old beliefs and am now free to experience peace and serenity.

CREATING MY NEW LIFE

In the previous section you started to see that the Universal Law of Mind acts on your beliefs to create your experiences. You began to identify and break free from negative patterns of belief and you are now aware of new possibilities. *Incorporating any additional understanding you gained in that section, write here what you want your new experience to be.*

_____

_____

_____

_____

This portion of the workbook will help you learn how to create an affirmative prayer to resolve your emotional concern. In affirmative prayer, you align your thinking with the Divine qualities of Peace and Serenity already inherent within you. When you do this, your experience changes. This change occurs as the Universal Law of Mind acts on your deeply held beliefs. (Remember, when we say "beliefs" we mean thoughts, feelings, and attitudes, both conscious and subconscious.)

Realizing through affirmative prayer that Peace and Serenity are the truth about God and that you are unified with God, you come to know that peace and serenity are also the truth about you in regard to emotional well-being. As a result, problems are resolved.

Each of the following exercises has two parts. The first part consists of an activity which helps prepare you to write your affirmative prayer. This activity is designed to assist you in developing an inner atmosphere of strong feeling and conviction, one that will make your statements effective. The second part involves actually writing the five stages of your affirmative prayer. Through this process, as you align your thinking with what is true about God, a solution to your emotional concern unfolds.

Each of the five stages of affirmative prayer — Recognition, Unification, Realization, Thanksgiving, and Release — is explained fully on the following pages: page 70 (Recognition), page 98 (Unification), page 126 (Realization), page 154 (Thanksgiving), and page 182 (Release). Examples are also provided. Be sure to refer to these examples for guidance and suggestions.

1 Become aware of the many expressions of a peaceful and serene Presence in the world. Birds singing, the sun rising or setting, clouds drifting across the sky — all of these are evidence of an abiding well-being around you. Recognizing the Peace and Serenity of God everywhere, become aware of the creative activity of God's Power in the world around you. Write in the space below what you think and feel about this Presence and Power.

_____

_____

_____

_____

_____

_____

_____

_____

_____

_____

There is a Presence and Power greater than you are — God — which is the Source and the Creator of everything around you. Recognize that there is one God, one Life, one Mind and that it is ever present, ever active, and constantly creative. Now state what you have recognized, letting your statement be as sincere and meaningful as you can.

_____

_____

_____

_____

_____

(See page 70 for examples of Recognition statements.)

2 As you observe the Presence and Power of God everywhere around you, begin now to experience your deep connection with God. Know you are part of God. Know there is one Life, that Life is God, and that Life is what you are. Know there is one Universal Law of Mind which always responds to your beliefs. Feel your oneness with the Divine qualities of Peace and Serenity, taking time to sense the presence of these qualities within you. When have you felt peaceful and serene? Remember these occasions and reflect on them. Become still and know that as a spiritual being you are not separate from these aspects of God-Life, nor are you separate from the Power that gives form to these aspects. Write in the space below what this experience of unification feels like.

Observing the Presence and the Power of God everywhere around you, become aware that you are part of a great Unity. Accept and feel your oneness with God. Make a statement below expressing how you experience your oneness with this Presence and Power greater than you are.

(See page 98 for examples of Unification statements.)

EMOTIONAL WELL-BEING

3 Maintaining a sense of your unity with a Presence and Power greater than you are, know that Peace and Serenity exist in place of your emotional concern. Contemplate this idea, ridding yourself of all doubt or reservation. Become deeply convinced that the new and positive experience you desire is unfolding for you. Record here the feelings you have as you do this.

Make a positive statement of your changed belief. Write it in the present tense, recognizing and accepting the presence of the Divine qualities of Peace and Serenity where your problem appears to be. You are creating a mold for the Universal Law of Mind, so be clear, definite, and specific. Be emphatic! Imagine that what you desire to experience is now established, knowing that it is already taking form in your life through the activity of the Universal Law of Mind. State here what you are now declaring to be true in place of your emotional concern.

(See page 126 for examples of Realization statements.)

4 Recall an occasion in your life when you felt a great outpouring of gratitude — whether for something specific or simply for the joy of being alive. Recapture in your imagination this special time of feeling grateful, and allow the experience to be fresh and vivid for you again. Describe here the feelings you have.

When you have an attitude of thanksgiving, knowing your need is already met, something in this attitude enhances your ability to have faith and to be open and receptive. Right now, completely and wholeheartedly accept that your emotional concern is resolved and feel thankful for this solution. Write a statement here expressing your gratitude.

(See page 154 for examples of Thanksgiving statements.)

EMOTIONAL WELL-BEING

5 Have you ever had the experience of feeling completely unburdened, as if a great weight had been lifted from your shoulders? What you felt was a letting go, a release. This is what you need to experience with respect to your emotional concern. Know that the Universal Law of Mind is now creating what you desire. Relax and experience a sense of trust, certain that this resolution is unfolding. Write below what the experience of release feels like.

Sometimes you may tend to doubt or deny the good you want to experience. The act of releasing your affirmative prayer helps prevent that. When you release it, the Universal Law of Mind can freely respond to your new spiritual understanding, revealing Peace and Serenity in place of your concern. Right now release all fear and worry, and allow this process to move forward. Let go of the problem and be confident that the good you desire is already unfolding. Write a statement releasing your affirmative prayer to the activity of the Universal Law of Mind.

(See page 182 for examples of Release statements.)

MY AFFIRMATIVE PRAYER

Taken together, the statements you have made at the bottom of the previous five pages comprise a complete affirmative prayer, addressing the particular emotional concern you have chosen to deal with. This prayer consists of the stages of Recognition, Unification, Realization, Thanksgiving, and Release.

Review each of your five statements now and determine if there are any changes you wish to make in them. As you review them, be sure they evoke deep feeling and conviction in you and are worded concisely for maximum impact. Also be sure they achieve the purpose intended. For example, when you reread your Realization statement, are you able to sense the Peace and Serenity of God in your life? After you make any desired changes in your five statements, combine them below into a complete unit.

1 Recognition:

2 Unification:

3 Realization:

4 Thanksgiving:

5 Release:

WHERE DO I GO FROM HERE?

You have now started a process of personal and spiritual growth that will produce new and positive changes for you.

You can do several things to continue the work you started in this section. Stay alert to the statements you make about your situation. At night recall your habitual thought patterns of the day. How much of your thinking was negative and how much was positive? Practice changing the negative statements into positive ones. Say the positive statements over and over until you begin to feel a definite connection with them.

Most important, read your affirmative prayer several times a day. At a minimum, we suggest doing so right before going to bed and upon waking in the morning. Read it out loud if possible. Take time to contemplate it. As you read your prayer and think about it, experience the feelings associated with each of the five stages. Be sure to make reading it meaningful, not simply an automatic exercise. If one of your statements seems to lose impact for you, redo it.

Remain open to change and be willing to follow any inner guidance that comes to you. God works in your life through such inner guidance, which often appears as a new idea or an urge to do something differently. As you allow change to occur, what was originally a problem will be replaced by more desirable circumstances. Remain open-minded and patient, knowing that positive results are certain to take place.

Remember, there is a natural process by which spiritual truth takes form, and the time this process requires varies with different situations. You may have an immediate response to your affirmative prayer or a period of weeks or even months may elapse, but continue with your affirmative prayer, always using the present tense, accepting that what you desire *is now happening*. Keep deepening your level of conviction and adjust the wording of your prayer to reflect your changed state of consciousness. Feel free to create new affirmations and affirmative prayers as your understanding of your unity with God's Peace and Serenity expands. Continue with your affirmative prayer until the desired result is obtained.

HOW AM I CHANGING?

Work with the "Old Patterns — New Possibilities" and "Creating My New Life" sections for two to three weeks, then respond to these questions. They will help you assess your progress and guide you if you need assistance. (Since keeping a record of your experiences is useful when you are seeking to improve your life, you may also want to write your continuing insights in a separate notebook.)

■ What changes have you experienced in your situation as a result of working with this section on emotional well-being?

_____

_____

_____

■ Are you satisfied with these results? If you are, what do you think is responsible for your improved circumstances?

_____

_____

_____

■ If you feel you are not making progress, go back over the questions and exercises and your responses to them. Do you need to do something differently? Also look at your affirmative prayer. Does it need to be changed? Be sure to check yourself on negative thought habits. Are you willing to reevaluate your approach and try again?

_____

_____

_____

■ What is the most important thing you have learned about yourself in regard to your emotional well-being?

_____

_____

_____

RELEASE

Release is the fifth stage of affirmative prayer. In this stage, after thankfully accepting your good as already accomplished, you release your prayer to the activity of the Universal Law of Mind, completely freeing yourself of concern.

Purpose of the Release stage of affirmative prayer: To mentally let go of your affirmative prayer and allow the Universal Law of Mind to work on it; to free yourself to act as though the good you are seeking is already present in your life.

Suggestions for creating an effective statement of release: In a statement of release, you completely let go of both your prayer and your concern about the problem. After you have completed the previous stages of your affirmative prayer, disconnect your thoughts from your problem and stop worrying about it. If you continue to have doubts or other negative thoughts, you have not completely released either your problem or your prayer. If such thoughts arise again in your mind, restate your release with as much conviction as you can command. Your release statement needs to be strong and specific, leaving you with the feeling that you have entirely let go of your affirmative prayer and are now trusting the activity of the Universal Law of Mind. Relax and know that you do not have to do anything further. Your work is done.

When you have reached the point of release in your mind and completely believe in it, make a definite, affirmative statement of release, turning your prayer over to the activity of God. Record your statement on the appropriate page of this workbook.

Examples of Release statements:

☐ Knowing that the Universal Law of Mind is now acting on my desire, I totally release all concern for the outcome, and I am at peace.

☐ I am fully convinced that the specific good I desire is now established as I release this affirmative prayer to the creative activity of the Universal Law of Mind.

☐ I joyfully let go of my affirmative prayer, knowing that God, through the activity of the Universal Law of Mind, is already creating the good I desire.

LIFE DIRECTION

We are born with a desire to love, to laugh, to sing, to dance, to create. Life is action, movement, and enthusiasm. This day in which we live, this hour, this moment is one from which we should distill all the joy there is, all the enthusiasm. — Ernest Holmes

Who am I? Why am I here? What is the meaning of life? If you are asking yourself these kinds of questions, you should know that in spite of any confusion you may be feeling, you are on the threshold of what can be a period of richly rewarding personal and spiritual growth.

Uncertainty about the direction, meaning, or purpose of life often comes at a time when you are ready for greater self-awareness — when you feel a need for a clearer perspective on who you are in relation to the world around you, to other people, and to God. This can be a time of profound self-discovery and renewal.

But it can also be a time of baffling and uncomfortable change. Your former way of life may not seem as satisfying to you as it once did. Certain goals and values, previously acceptable to you, may no longer feel right. Your entire world may even appear to be crumbling under your feet. In the midst of all this confusion and turmoil, however, you are likely to sense deep within yourself that a positive experience of growth and expansion is occurring — that Something within you is seeking greater expression.

This "Something" is your God-Self, the essence of your being, which is ever urging you toward a fuller expression of who you truly are. Through using affirmative prayer, you can open yourself to Guidance and Inspiration and find greater meaning in life. You can discover your unique purpose.

Begin now to recognize your unity with the Presence and Power of God. Affirm that your life is filled with worthwhile, rewarding activities and that you have a valuable contribution to make in the world. The Universal Law of Mind will respond to your direction by creating the meaningful life experience you desire. Take time to explore the possibilities open to you, using the exercises in the following sections to help you discover direction, purpose, and meaning in life.

OLD PATTERNS — NEW POSSIBILITIES

Old Patterns

Your beliefs — which include your thoughts, feelings, and attitudes, both conscious and subconscious — determine what you are now experiencing, for the Universal Law of Mind acts on them to create the circumstances of your life. Use the following exercises to help you become aware of the particular beliefs that underlie your difficulty with finding direction in your life. Take as much time as you need, perhaps a few days, to respond to these questions since they form an important foundation for the work you will be doing.

■ Look back at "Where Am I Now?" on the subject of life direction (page 26). If you haven't completed that exercise, please do so now. Use the space provided below to answer the following questions: What issues did you respond to with a number 3, 4, or 5? Are these issues related? If so, in what way? Select one of them to work with in this section and note it below.

■ Write down the feelings, especially the fears, you have in regard to this issue. What beliefs can you identify about yourself or about other people that underlie these feelings?

■ What new understanding has come to you as a result of exploring these old belief patterns? On the basis of your new understanding, what would you like to change?

_____

_____

_____

_____

_____

_____

_____

_____

New Possibilities

To break up old patterns of thought and behavior, you need to open yourself to new possibilities. The exercise on the following page, based on contrasting statements, will assist you with this process. Saying the statement in the left column first and then saying the statement in the right column will help you become aware of how you think, and also help you break up habitual non-productive patterns of thinking and expand your consciousness. (Create your own statements if the examples provided do not address your situation.)

When you affirm the statements in either the left or the right column, you are directing the activity of the Universal Law of Mind, which creates your experiences according to the patterns of your thoughts, feelings, and attitudes . . . your beliefs. If these beliefs are consistently negative, your experiences will be negative. If these beliefs are positive, your experiences will be positive. Remember, the Universal Law of Mind does not make choices — *you* make the choices through what you believe. *This means you can consciously choose how to direct the Universal Law of Mind to create the results you want.*

You will be working with these consciousness-expanders as a way of preparing for the next section, "Creating My New Life," in which you use affirmative prayer to deal with the need you have to find direction and meaning in your life. As you read each statement in the right column, see it as a new possibility. Imagine yourself being, acting, and feeling what it expresses. Believe it! Feel the feelings you would have if this statement were actually true right now. In this way you begin the process of changing your thinking.

How do you talk to yourself about your concern? How do you talk to others about it?

If you have been saying:

I'm not using my potential.

My life isn't going anywhere.

I don't have fun anymore.

There really isn't much to live for.

The days all seem the same to me.

My life doesn't have any direction.

I have trouble setting goals and accomplishing things.

I can't get enthusiastic about anything.

I don't feel needed.

I never do anything different.

I'm bored with everything.

I wish I could believe in God.

I'd like to change but I'm afraid.

I feel life is passing me by.

I quit my job and don't know what to do.

My life doesn't have any meaning.

I feel like a failure.

Making choices is hard for me.

I'm disillusioned with life.

I don't know what to do with my life.

Other_____

(use additional paper if necessary)

Now begin to say:

I find new ways to express my talents.

My life is filled with purpose and action.

I find ways to have fun.

I look forward to every new day with joy.

I sense the wonder of life each day.

I have a meaningful focus to my life.

I choose an interesting goal and look forward to reaching it.

I am enthusiastic and I enjoy life.

I am valued and needed.

I have new adventures all the time.

I find living fun and interesting.

I experience God in everything.

I accept change as part of a new life.

I participate fully in life.

I have exciting plans for each day.

I find meaning in everything.

Each day brings new opportunities.

I accept God's guidance in my life.

I make a difference in this world.

I have a clear sense of purpose.

_____

Now turn to the next section, "Creating My New Life," to learn to use affirmative prayer to deal with your need to find direction in your life.

DAILY AFFIRMATION:

I accept guidance and inspiration in my life.

CREATING MY NEW LIFE

In the previous section you started to see that the Universal Law of Mind acts on your beliefs to create your experiences. You began to identify and break free from negative patterns of belief and you are now aware of new possibilities. *Incorporating any additional understanding you gained in that section, write here what you want your new experience to be.*

_____

_____

_____

_____

This portion of the workbook will help you learn how to create an affirmative prayer to resolve your concern with finding direction for your life. In affirmative prayer, you align your thinking with the Divine qualities of Guidance and Inspiration already inherent within you. When you do this, your experience changes. This change occurs as the Universal Law of Mind acts on your new beliefs. (Remember, when we say "beliefs" we mean thoughts, feelings, and attitudes, both conscious and subconscious.)

Realizing through affirmative prayer that Guidance and Inspiration are the truth about God and that you are unified with God, you come to know that guidance and inspiration are also the truth about you in regard to meaning, purpose, and direction in your life. As a result, problems are resolved.

Each of the following exercises has two parts. The first part consists of an activity which helps prepare you to write your affirmative prayer. This activity is designed to assist you in developing an inner atmosphere of strong feeling and conviction, one that will make your statements effective. The second part involves actually writing the five stages of your affirmative prayer. Through this process, as you align your thinking with what is true about God, a solution to your concern regarding your life direction unfolds.

Each of the five stages of affirmative prayer — Recognition, Unification, Realization, Thanksgiving, and Release — is explained fully on the following pages: page 70 (Recognition), page 98 (Unification), page 126 (Realization), page 154 (Thanksgiving), and page 182 (Release). Examples are also provided. Be sure to refer to these examples for helpful suggestions.

I The perfect Presence and Power of God is everywhere and can be experienced as Guidance and Inspiration. The artist who paints a picture, the composer who writes a symphony, and the inventor who devises a new product are all drawing upon an ever-available source of inspiration. In nature, the many processes of life unfold with order and constancy, giving evidence of a guiding Intelligence within them. Recognizing the presence of Guidance and Inspiration everywhere, become aware of the creative activity of God's Power around you. Write in the space below what you think and feel about this Presence and Power.

There is a Presence and Power greater than you are — God — which is the Source and the Creator of everything around you. Recognize that there is one God, one Life, one Mind and that it is ever present, ever active, and constantly creative. Now state what you have recognized, letting your statement be as sincere and meaningful as you can.

(See page 70 for examples of Recognition statements.)

2 As you observe the Presence and Power of God everywhere around you, begin to experience your deep connection with God. Know you are part of God. Know there is one Life, that Life is God, and that Life is what you are. Know there is one Universal Law of Mind which always responds to your beliefs. Feel your oneness with the Divine qualities of Guidance and Inspiration, taking time to sense the presence of these qualities within you. When have you been particularly inspired or felt a clear sense of inner guidance? Remember these occasions and reflect on them. Become still and know that as a spiritual being you are not separate from God-Life, nor are you separate from the Power that gives form to Divine qualities. Write in the space below what this experience of unification feels like.

Observing the Presence and the Power of God everywhere around you, become aware that you are part of a great Unity. Accept and feel your oneness with God. Make a statement below expressing how you experience your oneness with this Presence and Power greater than you are.

(See page 98 for examples of Unification statements.)

3 Maintaining a sense of your unity with a Presence and Power greater than you are, know that Guidance and Inspiration are always available to help you find meaning and purpose in life. Contemplate this idea, ridding yourself of all doubt or reservation. Become deeply convinced that the new and positive experience you desire is unfolding for you. Record here the feelings you have as you do this.

Make a positive statement of your changed belief. Write it in the present tense, recognizing and accepting the presence of the Divine qualities of Guidance and Inspiration where your problem appears to be. You are creating a mold for the Universal Law of Mind, so be clear, definite, and specific. Be emphatic! Imagine that what you desire to experience is now established, knowing that it is already taking form in your life through the activity of the Universal Law of Mind. State here what you are now declaring to be true in place of your need for purpose and direction.

(See page 126 for examples of Realization statements.)

190

4 Recall an occasion in your life when you felt a great outpouring of gratitude — whether for something specific or simply for the joy of being alive. Recapture in your imagination this special time of feeling grateful, and allow the experience to be fresh and vivid for you again. Describe here the feelings you have.

When you have an attitude of thanksgiving, knowing your need is already met, something in this attitude enhances your ability to have faith and to be open and receptive. Right now, completely and wholeheartedly accept that your problem with finding purpose and meaning in life is resolved and feel thankful for this solution. Write a statement here expressing your gratitude.

(See page 154 for examples of Thanksgiving statements.)

5 Have you ever had the experience of feeling completely unburdened, as if a great weight had been lifted from your shoulders? What you felt was a letting go, a release. This is what you need to experience in regard to your need for direction and meaning in life. Know that the Universal Law of Mind is now creating what you desire. Relax and experience a sense of trust, certain that this resolution is unfolding. Write below what the experience of release feels like.

Sometimes you may tend to doubt or deny the good you want to experience. The act of releasing your affirmative prayer helps prevent that. When you release it, the Universal Law of Mind can freely respond to your new spiritual understanding, revealing the Guidance and Inspiration you seek. Right now release all fear and worry, and allow this process to move forward. Let go of the problem and be confident that the good you desire is already unfolding. Write a statement releasing your affirmative prayer to the activity of the Universal Law of Mind.

(See page 182 for examples of Release statements.)

MY AFFIRMATIVE PRAYER

Taken together, the statements you have made at the bottom of the previous five pages comprise a complete affirmative prayer, addressing your particular concern with life direction and meaning. This prayer consists of the stages of Recognition, Unification, Realization, Thanksgiving, and Release.

Review each of your five statements now and determine if there are any changes you wish to make in them. As you review them, be sure they evoke deep feeling and conviction in you and are worded concisely for maximum impact. Also be sure they achieve the purpose intended. For example, when you reread your Realization statement, are you able to sense the Guidance and Inspiration of God in your life? After you make any desired changes in your five statements, combine them below into a complete unit.

1 Recognition:

2 Unification:

3 Realization:

4 Thanksgiving:

5 Release:

WHERE DO I GO FROM HERE?

You have now started a process of personal and spiritual growth that will produce new and positive changes for you.

You can do several things to continue the work you started in this section. Stay alert to the statements you make about your situation. At night recall your habitual thought patterns of the day. How much of your thinking was negative and how much was positive? Practice changing the negative statements into positive ones. Say the positive statements over and over until you begin to feel a definite connection with them.

Most important, read your affirmative prayer several times a day. At a minimum, we suggest doing so right before going to bed and upon waking in the morning. Read it out loud if possible. Take time to contemplate it. As you read your prayer and think about it, experience the feelings associated with each of the five stages. Be sure to make reading it meaningful, not simply an automatic exercise. If one of your statements seems to lose impact for you, redo it.

Remain open to change and be willing to follow any inner guidance that comes to you. God works in your life through such inner guidance, which often appears as a new idea or an urge to do something differently. As you allow change to occur, what was originally a problem will be replaced by more desirable circumstances. Remain open-minded and patient, knowing that positive results are certain to take place.

Remember, there is a natural process by which spiritual truth takes form, and the time this process requires varies with different situations. You may have an immediate response to your affirmative prayer or a period of weeks or even months may elapse, but continue with your affirmative prayer, always using the present tense, accepting that what you desire *is now happening*. Keep deepening your level of conviction and adjust the wording of your prayer to reflect your changed state of consciousness. Feel free to create new affirmations and affirmative prayers as your understanding of your unity with God's Guidance and Inspiration expands. Continue with your affirmative prayer until the desired result is obtained.

HOW AM I CHANGING?

Work with the "Old Patterns — New Possibilities" and "Creating My New Life" sections for two to three weeks, then respond to these questions. They will help you assess your progress and guide you if you need assistance. (Since keeping a record of your experiences is useful when you are seeking to improve your life, you may also want to write your continuing insights in a separate notebook.)

■ What changes have you experienced in your situation as a result of working with this section on life direction?

_____

_____

_____

_____

■ Are you satisfied with these results? If you are, what do you think is responsible for your improved circumstances?

_____

_____

_____

_____

■ If you feel you are not making progress, go back over the questions and exercises and your responses to them. Do you need to do something differently? Also look at your affirmative prayer. Does it need to be changed? Be sure to check yourself on negative thought habits. Are you willing to reevaluate your approach and try again?

_____

_____

_____

■ What is the most important thing you have learned about yourself in regard to finding direction and meaning in your life?

_____

_____

_____

_____

SPIRITUAL MEDITATIONS

On the following pages are seven spiritual meditations adapted from the writings of Ernest Holmes. You may choose to read them in sequence throughout each week or, alternatively, to focus on those you find particularly meaningful. No matter which approach you take, we know you will be inspired by these readings and through using them daily you will become more fully conscious of your unity with the Presence and Power of God.

I Am Entering into a New Life

Today I am entering into a new life. The doorway of opportunity is open wide before me. Something within me is alert and aware. My will, my thought, and my imagination feel and sense new opportunities for self-expression. I identify myself with success. I am one with it. New ideas and new ways of doing things come to me.

I have complete confidence that I recognize opportunity when it presents itself. I know what to do under every circumstance and in every situation. There is a deep feeling within me that all is well. I am ready and willing to give the best I have to life, and I know the best that life has comes back to me.

Believing that Divine Power is back of every constructive thought, that I live in a Divine Presence which flows through everything, and that I am guided by an infinite Intelligence which knows everything, I live this day in complete assurance; I live this day in complete happiness. And I expect that every tomorrow will reveal an increasing unfoldment, an increasing revelation of that good which is eternally available for every person.

I Accept My Divine Birthright

I now accept my Divine birthright. I consciously enter into my partnership with Love, with Peace, with Joy, with God. I feel the infinite Presence close around me. I feel the warmth, the color, and the radiance of this Presence like a living thing in which I am enveloped.

I am no longer afraid of life. A deep and abiding sense of calm and poise flows through me. I have faith to believe that the Kingdom of God is at hand and that it is right where I am, here, now, today, at this moment.

I know there is a Universal Law of Mind which can, will, and does govern everything. I feel that everything in my thought which is life-giving, everything in my life which is constructive, is blessed and prospered.

I know there is a Presence which blesses everyone I meet. It makes glad every situation in which I find myself. It brings peace and comfort to everyone I contact. I am united with everything in life, in love, in peace, and in joy. And I know the Presence of Love and Life gently leads me and all others, guiding, guarding, sustaining, upholding — now and forever.

God Is at the Center of My Being

Believing that the Spirit of God is at the center of my being, I now let the Presence and Power of God go before me and prepare my way. Today I surrender all doubt and fear to this indwelling Presence. I release everything unlovely from my mind and permit love to fulfill its Divine purpose through me.

Realizing that God must be in all people, I permit the Divine Presence within me to greet the Divine Presence within others in glad recognition. Knowing that God must be in all people, I permit the God within me to reach out to everyone with a feeling of unity, of peace, and of understanding. Realizing that there can be but one Divine Presence in all things, I learn to feel and see it in everything I do.

I permit this Presence to govern and guide, to lead and direct my thoughts and my acts. Feeling that Love is the all-sustaining essence of life, the great Reality, I permit love to flow through me and embrace the whole world.

To the Divine Presence and to that Goodness which encircles all in its loving embrace, I commit myself now and forevermore.

Divine Power Is Operating Through Me Now

I know Divine Power is operating through me now. I know I am not limited by anything that has happened or by anything that is happening. I am aware that the Truth is making me free from any belief in want, lack, or limitation. I have a feeling of security and of ability to do any good thing I need to do.

I have complete confidence that the God who is always with me is able and willing to direct everything I do, to order my affairs, and to lead me into the pathway of peace and happiness. I free myself from every sense of condemnation, either against myself or others. I release every sense of animosity.

I am entering into an entirely new set of conditions and circumstances. That which has no limit is flowing through my consciousness into action. I am guided by the same Intelligence and inspired by the same Imagination which scatters the moonbeams across the waves and holds the forces of nature in its grasp. I have a calm, inward conviction of my union with good, my oneness with God.

I Am One with the Eternal Newness of Life

I realize I am one with the eternal newness of Life. My body is alive with the Life of God. My body is illumined by the Light of God. There is no darkness, discouragement, despair, or defeat. My mind is refreshed in the one Mind that eternally gives of itself to its creation.

I open my heart to accept the good gifts of joy, happiness, and enthusiasm, right now. I open my heart to know That which is forever ageless, and to know it is my Source.

Every part of my body is in harmony with the Divine Presence and Power within me. The Life of God flows through every atom of my being, vitalizing, invigorating, and renewing every part of my physical body.

I know that my body and my experiences reflect the image of Life in all of its newness, and I move through the days of my years with gladness in my mind. I dwell in the house of God forever, knowing that my cup is full to overflowing with the only life there is — the life and the eternal youth of God.

I Let God Guide Me

Today I let God guide me in everything I think, say, and do. I know I am rightly guided and I know what to do under every circumstance.

Today I permit the Life of God to energize every atom of my being, knowing that the food I eat, the thoughts I think, and the faith I have are converted into living, radiant substance.

Today I let the gladness of God flow through me, making glad everything I do and everyone I contact. I permit the Love of God to flow from me to all people, embracing them in one universal family, which is the household of God.

Today I open my mind to the influx of new ideas, knowing that God makes all things new. New thoughts, new ideas, new people, new circumstances come into my experience as I draw upon the invisible forces of my own being — the Love and the Life, the Peace and the Joy — the forces which are of God, the living Spirit Almighty.

God Is All the Presence There Is

Believing that God is all the Presence there is, I feel this Presence in everything and in everyone. Dwelling on the thought that God is Love, I permit my mind to become filled with the consciousness of this Love. I permit this Love to envelop everything and everyone, knowing it brings a sense of peace and joy and certainty.

Realizing that God is Life, I open my thought to such a complete inflowing of this Divine Life that I see it and feel it everywhere — the one perfect Life which is God — in people, in nature, animating every act, sustaining all movement. My faith in this Life is complete, positive, and certain.

Knowing that all things are possible to faith, I say to my own mind: Be not afraid. Faith makes my way certain. Faith goes before me and prepares the way.

Believing God is in everyone, I meet God in people and sense my unity with everyone I meet. Knowing God is Peace, I open my mind to the quiet influence and the calm certainty of Peace. Knowing God is Joy, I meet every situation in happiness. Recognizing that the Presence and Power within me can do all things with complete assurance, I let God guide me always into a greater experience of love and good.

FOR FURTHER READING

The following materials comprise a selective bibliography of writings by and about Ernest Holmes and are recommended to those readers interested in learning more about the Science of Mind philosophy.

Books by Ernest Holmes:

Good for You. Los Angeles, Science of Mind Publications, 1987. This compilation of selected writings by Ernest Holmes contains a definitive explanation of affirmative prayer, along with a number of spiritual mind treatments (affirmative prayers) for dealing with specific needs.

How to Change Your Life. Los Angeles: Science of Mind Publications, 1982. This concise and readable presentation of the basic concepts of the Science of Mind philosophy is thorough yet easy to understand. Especially helpful to the beginner, it includes instructions for using Science of Mind principles.

*How to Use the Science of Mind. New York: G. Putnam's Sons, 1948. Ideal for serious students who want to expand their ability to apply Science of Mind principles, this practical volume contains explanations of many concepts basic to spiritual mind treatment (affirmative prayer).

*The Science of Mind. New York: G. Putnam's Sons, 1938. This profound book has brought spiritual understanding to thousands of people throughout the world. The authoritative text-book for teaching the Science of Mind, it is a monumental work which you will refer to again and again as your own understanding deepens.

*This Thing Called Life. New York: G. Putnam's Sons, 1943. Based upon the ideas of some of the world's great spiritual leaders and philosophers, this classic book on the Science of Mind teaches the building and practice of faith. It includes powerful affirmations as well as a basic explanation of spiritual mind treatment (affirmative prayer).

*This Thing Called You. New York: G. Putnam's Sons, 1948. Through its simple and direct approach, this inspiring book helps you deepen your understanding of who you are and also assists you in putting the life-changing concepts of the Science of Mind to work in your life.

Ideas for Living. Los Angeles: Science of Mind Publications, 1979. These fifteen thoughtful essays discuss a range of topics central to the Science of Mind philosophy. They are particularly useful in helping you discover and develop the power of your own thought.

Living Without Fear. Los Angeles: Science of Mind Publications, 1962. This book focuses on how to use Science of Mind principles to free yourself from the problems and limitations that result from fear.

Practical Application of Science of Mind. Los Angeles: Science of Mind Publications, 1958. These powerful ideas, based on the premise that thought is creative, provide help in understanding the Science of Mind philosophy as well as in applying its concepts to your daily life.

---

*Also available on audio cassette tape from Science of Mind Publications

Books by Other Authors:

Addington, Jack. *The Secret of Healing*. Los Angeles: Science of Mind Publications, 1979. This inspiring book is a valuable resource for developing greater insight into the value of affirmative prayer.

Carter, Craig. *How To Use the Power of Mind*. Los Angeles: Science of Mind Publications, 1948. This comprehensive handbook offers help in dealing with a wide range of personal concerns. It includes explanations of basic Science of Mind principles, along with a number of spiritual mind treatments (affirmative prayers) to use for resolving these concerns.

Holmes, Fenwicke. *Ernest Holmes: His Life and Times*. New York: G. Putnam's Sons, 1970. This inspiring biography describes the influences and events that shaped the life of a man who was not only a great spiritual leader but also a loving and courageous human being.

Hornaday, William H.D. and Harlan Ware. *Your Aladdin's Lamp*. Los Angeles: Science of Mind Publications, 1979. These warm, personal stories present intimate portraits of Ernest Holmes and others whose lives are proof of what conscious and constructive use of the power of thought can achieve.

Niendorff, John S. *Listen to the Light*. Los Angeles: Science of Mind Publications, 1980. These thought-provoking and poetic writings originally appeared in *Science of Mind* Magazine as the first fifty-four "Cornerstone" essays. With clarity, insight, and originality, the author explores many fascinating dimensions of the new consciousness.

Seabury, David. *Release from Your Problems*. Los Angeles: Science of Mind Publications, 1966. This book helps you understand that your problems carry valuable messages from your inner self and that when you learn to interpret these messages correctly, you will experience greater joy and fulfillment in life.

Stortz, Margaret. *Start Living Every Day of Your Life*. Los Angeles: Science of Mind Publications, 1981. This collection of over eighty power-packed meditations will bring you both immediate assistance and enduring inspiration.

Periodicals:

Science of Mind Magazine. Los Angeles: Science of Mind Publications. This popular, internationally circulated monthly publication, founded by Ernest Holmes in 1927, includes interviews, articles, daily self-help meditations, and other regular features which teach and inspire.

Science of Mind Publications
3251 West Sixth Street
P.O. Box 75127
Los Angeles, California 90075

Ernest Holmes (1887-1960), who developed the philosophy on which this workbook is based, is known internationally as one of this century's outstanding spiritual teachers. A lifelong student of philosophy and religion, he developed a practical approach to successful living — the Science of Mind — which combines his own spiritual insight with essential principles of the world's enduring religious beliefs.

Holmes wrote many books, including his classic *The Science of Mind*. He also founded *Science of Mind* Magazine and the United Church of Religious Science. Through his lectures, study courses, radio and television programs, tape recordings, and books and other publications, he introduced millions of people to the life-changing concepts of the Science of Mind philosophy.

ABOUT THE AUTHORS

Mary M. Jaeger, Ph.D., is an educator, communications specialist, and Religious Science minister. As Director of Research and Development at Ernest Holmes College, she creates programs and materials that teach the Science of Mind philosophy.

Kathleen Juline, M.S.L.S., J.D., is Senior Editor of *Science of Mind* Magazine and co-editor of the book *Good for You,* a compilation of selected writings by Ernest Holmes.